INTUITIVE REIKI

*A transformational journey of
deep spiritual awakening*

LISA BRANDIS

Copyright © Lisa Brandis, 2023

All rights reserved.

ISBN (print): 978-0-6488988-1-8
ISBN (ebook): 978-0-6488988-0-1

Publisher's Note:
This is a work of nonfiction. Some names have been changed to protect their privacy. This work depicts actual events in the life of the author as truthfully as recollection permits, and where dialogue was used, the author has made every attempt possible to capture the essence and emotion of the conversations as accurately as possible. Although Lisa is a Reiki Master and Clinical Hypnotherapist, the information in this book is general in nature and should not be used as a substitute for the advice of a clinical psychologist, doctor or any medical practitioner.

The advice and strategies found within may not be suitable for every person or situation. This work is sold with the understanding that neither the author nor the publisher are held responsible for how people choose to use the information or advise received from this book.

Cover Design: Damonza.com
Print and eBook Formatting: Damonza.com
Author Photos: Simone Lee
Editing: Eileen Cullan and Susanne Bellamy
Proofreading: Robyn Martin
Publishing Coach: Athena Daniels

No part or the whole of this book may be reproduced, stored in a retrieval system, distributed, transmitted or utilized (other than for reading by the intended reader) in ANY form (now known or hereafter invented) without prior written permission by the author. The unauthorised reproduction or distribution of this copyrighted work is illegal, and punishable by law.

Disclaimer

The stories and concepts that I share in this book are not meant to change your beliefs or philosophy of life, nor are they meant to be accepted as truth. I write about my experiences with Reiki in the hope that it will inspire within you a desire to deepen your own understanding of the spirit within through the sharing of my thoughts, visions, experiences and ideas. Over the years of practising Reiki, I have seen that the way in which Reiki is practised is as varied, individual and unique as we are. While the energy that moves with and through us all is the same light, how it inspires us to teach is unique and sacred. It is with great respect for all forms and lineages of Reiki that I share my story with you in hope that it might awaken a spark within you to learn more.

It is my sincere desire that all who are touched by the magic of Reiki also find their way back home to their sacred heart.

Dedication

This book is dedicated to my husband Gerald, thank you for always loving me, just the way I am. You enrich my life in so many ways. My daughters Georgia and Hannah. Thank you for being such vibrant and passionate spirits; your kind and loving hearts make the world a better place. It is my greatest joy to be your mother and to share in this beautiful life with you both.

Praise for Intuitive Reiki

'This book is written from the heart, a beautifully delivered account of Lisa's discovery and subsequent journey to find her magic. Her openness in sharing her experiences showed her vulnerability and an honesty I could relate to. Reading Lisa's book gave me confirmation of my own intuition and experiences that I was having when doing my reiki sessions for others. Many ah-ha moments were had! I highly recommend this book to anyone searching for more insights into the mysteries and magic of our souls journeys and how to connect to the wisdom we all have inside us.'

Fiona Greenlaw: 5 Stars

'Intuitive Reiki is not just another book about Reiki. Lisa shares her own very personal & often vulnerable healing story, whilst weaving in her expansive love of and the power of Reiki. Lisa has created a beautiful tapestry which brings together the threads of her personal journey, which often resonates with our own life struggles and personal awareness. Everyone's Reiki journey is unique and in sharing some of her own experiences, Lisa provides useful knowledge and practical techniques which are a helpful guide for anyone wanting to expand their own connection with self and Source energy. "Intuitive Reiki" gently touches the heart space in us all, where we seek and find, deeper insight and self-healing. Tune into your heart right now, because I'm sure that it's telling you that this book has been written for you.'

Julie Teshome: 5 stars

'Lisa shares with us her beautiful life's journey of helping others. A genuine and heartfelt book, including deeply personal stories that will tug your heart and restore your faith in the generosity of people. Not only does this book introduce people to Reiki, Spirit and Intuition. It also provides practical examples and principals on how we all can reconnect back to our heart, intuition and purpose and immerse them within our daily lives improving connections with each other and loved ones. Highly recommend I loved reading this book!'

Robyn Martin: 5 Stars

Contents

Disclaimer iii
Dedication v
Praise for Intuitive Reiki vi
Introduction xii
1: Early Beginnings 1
   Being Captain Starlight *1*
   Beautiful Brittany Fairy *3*
   Wrapped in a Blanket of Love *10*
   Synchronicity - A Joyful Reward from Spirit *11*
   Cigarettes, Self-Love & the Divine *14*
2: What is Reiki? 21
   History & Background *21*
   The Practice of Reiki *22*
   Integration of Reiki into Healthcare *23*
   Intuitive Knowing & the Ego *23*
   What is Intuitive Reiki? *25*
   Principles of Reiki *26*
   Attunements and Symbols *34*
   Holding Space *37*
   Soul Mates & Living the Principles *38*
   Our Happiness Bubble Burst *40*
3: Understanding Emotions and Thoughts 47
   Emotions and Intuition *47*
   Being the Observer *52*
   Power of Your Mind *56*

4: The Next Step 59
Answering the Call from Spirit *59*
The Transformative Power of Reiki *64*
Awakening Psychic Abilities *65*
Introducing Intuitive Reiki International *67*

5: Living from the Heart. 71
The Science of the Heart. *71*
The Heart and Intuitive Reiki *72*
The Power of Touch *75*
Power vs Force *76*

6: Beyond the Basics 81
Grounding Your Energy *81*
White Lighting *82*
More than Running Energy *83*
In the Presence of Love *84*
Working with Christ Light *86*
Attuned with the Christ Consciousness *88*
Love vs Fear *89*
Soul Awareness *92*
Source Energy vs Psychic Energy *94*
Healing Connections *97*

7: Personal Growth from Reiki 99
Surrender *99*
Psychic Protection, Self-Love and Light *101*
Listen to Your Body *105*
The Hidden Meaning Behind Your Ring Finger *107*
Where Attention Goes, Energy Flows *108*
Thoughts Create Your Reality *110*
Powerful Positive Intention *112*

8: Exploring the Spirit World 115
Connecting to Spirit *115*
Meeting Anya and My Spirit Team *118*
What is Channelling? *123*

Channelling Messages from Anya *126*
Developing Trust in Channelling *127*
9: Changing Lives with Intuitive Reiki 133
Kaitlyn. *134*
Candy *135*
Linda. *137*
Amber *139*
Acknowledgments. 142
Index 145
About the Author 147

Introduction

As a professional intuitive and spiritual teacher who's been practicing for more than twenty years, I've spent most of my life helping people trust their intuition through the practice of Reiki. When we trust our vibes, we access powerful guidance from within that leads us to discover and fulfil our life's purpose, leading to greater happiness and contentment.

Knowing what I know today, my spiritual journey began before I was born and remained a mystery until I was twenty-three years old. Since then, significant life events led me on a search to find more meaning in my life and to gain insights on how I could live a more empowered life and assist others in the same way. This journey gradually led me to the practice of Reiki, which has had a profound and life-changing effect on me as well as thousands of students that I have personally taught over the past two decades.

I have great respect for all Reiki masters, mentors and teachers, and although Reiki is the foundation of my teaching, this is not just another Reiki book. Rather, in this book I will share with you how becoming a Reiki Master led me to open my heart, create deep, meaningful connections with others and answer the call of my inner knowing – skills that would help me through some of the most terrifying and heart-breaking experiences. I will also share how to tap into and trust your intuition so that you can be your most beautiful, authentic self and live an empowered life.

As you journey through these pages it is my hope that you will receive answers to some of life's biggest questions, such as: *Can everyone access their intuition? If so, how? Is there something greater than what we see and experience in the physical plane? What is spirit? Is there life after death?*

I also hope that by giving you an insight into Intuitive Reiki, and how it can enhance your connection to the spiritual realm, you will feel inspired to embark on the journey with me.

I have experienced so many miracles, big and small, throughout my Reiki journey. As Marianne Williamson describes, "A miracle is a shift in perception from fear to love—from a belief in what is not real, to faith in that which is. That shift in perception changes everything." This is what Reiki did for me and it is my desire that by reading this book you will feel the call to connect with the powerful presence of love within.

EARLY BEGINNINGS

Being Captain Starlight

My spiritual journey began when I was twenty-three years old. I landed a really cool job, one that would change the course of my whole life. I had been studying and acting since I was in high school (with some small success, but I'll share more about that later in the book), and this job was my dream job. It was at the Princess Margaret Children's Hospital in Perth, Western Australia. I was to be the first female Captain Starlight in Perth, with the delightful role of brightening the lives of seriously ill children. In addition to my role as Captain Starlight, I was appointed to be the Assistant Manager of the Starlight Express Room (SER), a bright and colourful room located on the top floor of the hospital, as well as the host of the Starlight TV Program.

I first worked alongside a man called Otto Kamenzin who was a very charismatic character. I had a little crush on him, however I was too professional to let him know, although I'm sure he had his suspicions. Working with Otto was fun; he had a smile that would light up the entire room, and a spirit that was larger than life. Both Otto and I would entertain the children via live streaming from the SER to a TV above the children's hospital beds, playing games and having fun and laughing at ourselves and each other. As Captain Starlight I learned how to paint faces, do magic tricks, make funny videos, tell stories and have live chats on the phone with children who couldn't make it into the SER because they were too unwell. I did many crazy things, all for the sake of making the children laugh and adding a little joy into their day. Once I even did the chicken dance on the side of a main road to fits of giggles from the children watching me from the window of the SER. Even though the children viewed me as their "super friend," I in turn, felt so extremely blessed to interact and spend time with these children. It was a joy-filled time in my life, and one I reflect on with great appreciation, especially now while writing this book.

So, what does Starlight have to do with intuition and Reiki? This is the time where my Reiki journey began. If it wasn't for the role of Captain Starlight, I don't think I would have heard the call to learn, practise, and eventually become a Reiki Master.

I began the journey as Captain Starlight because of my talents as an actor, but it gifted me with so much more experience than that. In fact, when I started working at Starlight, I remember my mum having some concerns. I'm very sensitive and empathic, and back then she thought the job would be emotionally difficult for me. While it was at times, the job mostly opened and expanded my heart in so many profound and beautiful ways. At Starlight, I often found myself talking with parents, children and staff who were vulnerable and feeling emotional. While some may have found it challenging to interact with them, I quite naturally knew exactly what to say, which often left them feeling lighter and uplifted. It became clear to me that sometimes the greatest gift we can give to another is our time, attention, compassion and love. Over time, I realised the difference I could make in their lives. But more significantly, making that difference was such a natural and easy thing for me to do. This was the birthplace of my intuition - the opening of my heart, and my desire to be of service to others.

Our team at Starlight grew to approximately twenty volunteers with whom I had the pleasure of working alongside. Getting to know them, the children and their families was one of the most rewarding parts of my job. I met some incredibly strong and beautiful families who, over time, would expand my heart to hold a greater love than I ever thought possible, and put me directly in touch with my soul's greater purpose.

Beautiful Brittany Fairy

I met and entertained so many incredible children, but there was one very special young girl, Brittany, who had Acute Myeloid Leukaemia, which is a type of cancer that affects the bone and blood marrow.

She was the most adorable little angel I'd ever met. Her totally gorgeous smile and giggle would melt hearts. Her parents, Debbie and Tim, were kind and warm-hearted people who I got to know very well over the nine months Brittany was in hospital. Because the family was from a small country town outside of Perth, they stayed in the Ronald McDonald House located across the road from the hospital, and, as a result, spent a lot of time with us in the SER. Otto and I frequently talked about how adorable Brittany was. "She totally reminds me of the cutest little fairy," I said to Otto. "She even looks like one," he replied. Like most of the children we worked with, Brittany had lost her hair due to the chemotherapy treatment she had been receiving. Despite the hair loss, we saw all the children as adorable and so easy to love for their bright little personalities; I thought it allowed their beautiful features to shine through. We often reminded ourselves that we had the best job in the world.

One day when Otto was in Fremantle, he found a statue of a fairy and mentioned to the store owner that it reminded him of Brittany. Otto relayed to the store owner, "There is a patient in the hospital called Brittany and she is the most adorable child. Her little face lights up the room when she smiles, and she has been so brave and endured many painful treatments for her leukaemia. When I look at this fairy, it totally reminds me of her." The store owner was deeply inspired by the story of Brittany and, as a result, offered to donate the statue of the fairy to Otto and Starlight in honour of little Brittany. Otto walked into the SER with a statue which stood approximately 40 centimetres tall in his arms, and my heart skipped a beat, as seeing a big strong man holding the most beautiful angel in his arms was not what I was expecting. I asked him, "Where did you get that fairy?" Otto told me what had happened at the fairy shop. Then he said, "Why don't we name the fairy after Brittany? We'll call her the Brittany Fairy." We agreed that it would make a great statue for the Starlight Express Room. We invited Tim, Brittany's dad, to come and have a look and after some discussion, Tim had an amazing idea. "Why don't I make a donation box and we can put the fairy on top…that way, people can donate to Starlight so that you can continue helping others like you have helped our family," he said. Space was made and our sparkly new Brittany Fairy was located just inside the SER to be the first thing people saw when they walked into the room.

A week later Tim brought in a beautifully crafted wooden donation box to be placed under the statue. I also took a photo of Brittany and her family and placed it on the side of the box so that people could see the beautiful girl who had inspired the donation box. We then held a ceremony with her parents, the state manager of Starlight, senior management, volunteers, staff and other patients to commemorate the placement of this very special piece. We received many generous donations. Although loose change was often donated, it wasn't uncommon to find $50 and $20 notes in the box. Over the years, the Brittany Fairy raised a considerable amount of money for the Starlight Children's Foundation and its programs.

A few months after the Brittany Fairy was erected, word came to us that Brittany was unwell and had been moved to the Intensive Care Unit (ICU) of the hospital. I often visited the cancer ward on my rounds, and on this day, I knocked on Brittany's hospital door and entered the room to find Brittany lying quietly, cuddled against her mother's chest. There were few words spoken, as I knew that Brittany was sharing a very personal moment with her mum; Brittany was lying across her mother's arms with her little legs dangling off to the side. She had her head resting on her mum's chest and was fast asleep. She looked so comfortable and peaceful resting in her mother's arms. Seeing an eight-year-old girl being cradled like a baby, however, was too much for me to bear; it broke my heart. While all other children her age were running around playing and having fun, there was Brittany, resting in the love and comfort of her mother's arms, experiencing a moment of peace from the pain and discomfort of this debilitating disease that was ravishing her frail body.

Not wanting to disturb Brittany and her mother, I whispered, "I'll come back later." But Debbie motioned for me to sit next to her on the bed and said, "It's okay, Lisa, you can stay. I'd like the company." I sat with them offering my time, presence and company. We quietly spoke and savoured the feeling of love that embraced the three of us. I can't recall what we spoke about on that day as it was so long ago, but what I experienced and felt in that hospital room was something that changed me forever. It was a feeling that surrounded me, as if I had walked into a room filled with 100,000 angels (although back then I didn't see clairvoyantly as I do now). I felt immense unconditional love; the kind of love I would later experience for myself when I became a mother and gave birth to my two beautiful daughters, first Georgia and then Hannah. The energy I felt that day moved me to the core of my being and something shifted within me in that moment. It's hard to put it into words, but it was a feeling of such reverence and love, which I still feel as strongly now as I did back then.

Beautiful Brittany took her last breath a few days later, and grief hit all of us who cared for her like a ton of bricks. I was devastated by her death. We lost not only Brittany on that day, but her family as well. They moved away from the hospital and back to the small town they lived in to heal and begin the next part of their lives. To this day, when I think about Brittany's family, I am filled with so many beautiful and positive memories.

Given I was only in my twenties, I had not yet experienced the loss of someone I was close to, let alone a child too young to leave this world. I had a broken heart. Although my mum heard many of the stories and experiences while I was at Starlight, this was exactly what my mum was concerned about. I cried in my mum's arms and told her how confused I was. I didn't understand the world anymore. I had more questions than answers. My mum felt my pain too. She placed a fairy statue of her own in her back garden as a reminder of the joy Brittany brought into all our lives. She had also made the most beautiful quilt for Brittany, which I gave to Debbie when Brittany was transferred to ICU. I have since been told that the quilt was passed down to Brittany's sister's first-born daughter, Olivia, who at the time of writing this book, was twenty-months-old.

My sadness soon turned to frustration. I needed answers which I wasn't getting, and so I became angry at God. I couldn't understand why God would take such a gorgeous little girl away from the world and from her family. I was feeling such grief and could only imagine what it must have been like for her family. On reflection I wanted someone to blame, because in my world, this didn't make any sense. Growing up, I was taught that if we are kind and do good things, then all will be okay. Bad things happen to bad people. Now I know that's very basic, but sometimes the beliefs that we hold are just that - basic ideas that are mostly formed when we are very young, but which are the foundations of who we become.

For two months I struggled with Brittany's death, and so I decided to seek the help of a psychologist. I had a few therapy sessions and shared with the psychologist questions I had going around and around in my head: *Why do such things happen to which there are no answers? Why did she get sick? Why so young? Why do some recover and some don't?*

My therapist stated that there were no answers to those questions, and what it really represented was my frustration that she had died. Through therapy, I later discovered that one of the other reasons I felt so strongly was because Brittany's family reminded me of my own family. My dad, Andy, has a heart of gold, and is one of the kindest men I know. And my mum, Naomi, is a strong and deeply loving woman who raised me to be the confident and happy woman that I now am. I am so blessed to have been raised by such loving parents. Although I accepted the anger I felt, I still had a deep yearning to understand life and death on a deeper level, and so my search continued. It didn't take long before the Universe answered.

This was the moment Reiki entered my life.

Shortly after Brittany's death, I had been given a dream opportunity. Starlight was flying me to Sydney to spend a week at a training conference at the prestigious acting school, the National Institute for Dramatic Art (NIDA).

Only a small number of people were accepted annually, so in my mind, anyone who went to that school had already made it; being accepted there meant you had talent and the 'x factor' that can't be learned, but is a part of one's being. To give you some idea of what that meant to me, I had auditioned for five consecutive years to enrol in the three-year Bachelor of Arts program in Acting at the Western Australia Academy of Performing Arts (WAAPA) and NIDA, only to be rejected each time. Instead, I attended classes at the Film and Television Institute in Perth, which in turn, ended up being an amazing experience. So here I was nearly a decade later, attending a workshop at NIDA, and I was elated. Then, right before my trip, my acting agent called me to tell me that I had been given a small extra part on the very popular Australian show at the time, *All Saints*. To say I was excited was an understatement.

I spent the week at NIDA and had an absolute ball, hanging out, expanding on my acting and entertaining skills with fellow Captain Starlights from around the country. Then the day before I was meant to be on the set of *All Saints*, my agent rang me and said, "Lisa, I'm so sorry but the network has cancelled your spot on *All Saints*. The casting director just told me they overbooked extras and therefore, don't need you on set tomorrow. I am so sorry Lisa; I know how disappointed you must feel."

She was right. I'd been looking forward to this day for months, and was shocked and extremely disappointed. Consequently, I spiralled into a negative spin, and felt both physically and emotionally exhausted. All the negative emotions I had been suppressing bubbled to the surface. I was experiencing my first emotional burnout.

Wrapped in a Blanket of Love

I was staying at my Auntie Pauline's house in Sydney with her friend, Susan Warland who, seeing my distress, asked if I would like to receive Reiki. Although I had never heard of Reiki, Susan was so kind, and I was open to anything at that stage, so I accepted her invitation. I sat on a dining chair in the middle of Pauline's lounge room and received my first Reiki session.

My first experience of Reiki felt like I was being wrapped in a blanket of invisible love. I felt all the physical stress and tension literally dissolve from my body, and in its place came an energy of gentle relaxation and relief, followed by a feeling of deep peace. I told Susan that I could feel waves of energy being released through the soles of my feet, to which she said, "Great, let it all go, Lisa." The tears gently flowed as I surrendered and let go, allowing healing to take place. When Susan stopped running Reiki and I had a chance to gather my thoughts, I realised how much lighter I felt, physically, mentally, and emotionally.

After that first session, I was intrigued and wanted to learn more about Reiki. With that in mind, I joined Susan's family on a little holiday they had planned. I received Reiki daily and noticed so many things in my life improving, mostly physical in those early days. I slept all night and had more energy in my body. I felt my body align and restore.

At the time I wanted to be anyone but myself. Many of the people who I admired were happy and confident. They would walk in a room and light it up. They knew who they were and had a sense of strength about them. In contrast, I felt very insecure and overly emotional. I loved acting and felt such passion about being an actor, but I was also so afraid that I wasn't good enough, and I spent way too much of my time comparing myself to others. In my own opinion, I just didn't measure up. But the powerful pull to be an actor remained. In my spare time I auditioned for acting parts, but was continually rejected. Although rejection is part of being an actor, it served to reinforce my belief that I wasn't good enough, again and again. Over time, however, I learned to move through the rejection with more ease. I had spent my life looking outward, making judgements about myself as I compared myself to everyone else. And yet, there was this amazing, smart, beautiful girl within me that I did not know, let alone understand, and never thought to love. And so it began. With my passion ignited, I decided that when I returned to Perth, I would learn Reiki.

Synchronicity - A Joyful Reward from Spirit

It didn't take me long to realise that when you are in alignment with your life purpose, all manner of magical things starts to happen. On my first day back at work I bumped into my volunteer coordinator, Vicki Hobbs, and a new volunteer named Vanessa, who had the biggest, most beautiful smile. I immediately thought that this girl was going to be fun. As it turned out, she was a Reiki practitioner.

"I love Reiki. I have just experienced a few sessions while I was away and I couldn't get enough," I said.

"I'd love to give you Reiki, let me know when you would like a session," Vanessa said.

"How about right now?" I asked with a great big grin

on my face. And without hesitating, Vanessa agreed to do so, stating that the best thing about Reiki is that it can be done anywhere. As we made our way across the carpark to the Starlight room, Vanessa shared how she discovered Reiki and explained some of its basic principles. Once inside the Starlight room, we sat on one of the rainbow-coloured cubes. Vanessa gently placed her hands first on my shoulders and then on my back, and began to give me Reiki. I took a deep breath and as I started to relax, I felt a familiar feeling of expansive peace. "Your hands are so hot," I said. "That's the Reiki energy you feel," Vanessa replied.

I felt instantly drawn into the fullness of the present moment by the Reiki energy, and my visual perspective expanded. As I sat in front of the great big windows that lined the Starlight room, an incredible view stretched out before me. With a new-found sense, I began to really see and appreciate how beautiful the scenery was. I noticed the trees, the people walking across the carpark, the cars moving, everyone and everything moving. I could see across the landscape of the city of Perth to the Perth hills. I could see far and wide in the distance. It was surreal. It felt like I had entered a beautiful vortex in which time slowed. I became aware of my body, the simplicity of my breath, and being present. And at the same time, I was overcome by a feeling of ecstatic peace.

The energy I felt was recognisable to my mind and my body. It felt very similar to my first experience with Reiki at my auntie's house. However, this time I was more aware of the sensations in my body. I felt a rush of intense heat that was both powerful and nurturing at the same time. I felt a connection growing between Vanessa and me that was unusual; it was as if Reiki began to bond us in an instant kinship, which later grew into a beautiful friendship. The experience lasted about ten minutes, and as soon as it was over, I was full of questions for the lovely Vanessa, which she was happy to answer.

Vanessa continued to share with me the basics of Reiki and told me how it had completely changed her life. She then introduced me to her Reiki Master, Jacqueline Tuffnell, who would go on to support me in moving through fear-based thoughts and beliefs, and to teach me to accept and love myself. Much to everyone's surprise, she inspired me to have a complete career change. And so, my lifelong journey with Reiki took another step.

I often wonder about the many ways the Universe supports us, especially when we are walking in the direction of our soul's calling. I'd never heard of Reiki before my week at NIDA, and it's most likely that at the time, not many others had either. To have been in Sydney experiencing Reiki the week before, and then to be introduced to a new volunteer who happened to be a Reiki practitioner many years before Reiki was a household name, was an amazing coincidence. I don't believe in coincidences anymore. I now call them *synchronicities,* which is the Universe's way of letting us know we are on the right path. I often think it's like we're little sail boats on the great ocean of life, and the soul is the wind gently adding power when we are heading in the right direction for our own soul's evolution and ultimate happiness. I was so excited at the prospect of learning Reiki, I phoned Jacqueline, and within a month I was booked in to learn the first level of Reiki.

Take a moment now to look back over your life. Have

you had profound and pivotal moments where it felt like everything lined up easily and effortlessly, or you just happened to be in the right place at the right time? I know that I have had many, and the more I am open to the messages from my soul, the more my life seems to flow with ease and grace. I like to think of it as having a spiritual GPS.

Cigarettes, Self-Love & the Divine

I remember the day I met Jacqueline as though it was yesterday. Jacqueline lived and worked from the most divine property in Roleystone, Perth. *Edenlight Retreat* was stunning. Her large house sat atop a hill and was surrounded by giant majestic trees and native foliage of Australia. As I drove my little white hatchback up the windy driveway and parked on top of the hill, I was in awe of the most breathtaking views of nature across the valley that spanned as far as my eyes could see. I soon came to love all the many blessings that nature provides us. From that day on, I looked forward to every visit to *Edenlight Retreat*; it felt nurturing to drive out of the hustle and bustle of the city and up the hill to her property, which beckoned me to enjoy a brand new and uplifting experience.

So, there I was in my little car, finishing a cigarette. I had been a smoker for ten years and never thought about quitting as taking care of my health wasn't a priority back then. I enjoyed smoking, especially during weekends hanging out with friends who also smoked. I also relied on the habit when I felt sad, stressed or angry. It was clear I was addicted. However, while sitting outside of *Edenlight*

Retreat, little did I know that my smoking days were coming to an end thanks to Reiki.

I meandered my way down a beautiful garden path to find Jacqueline waiting for me outside her double glass doors. She greeted me with a very warm smile and a great big motherly hug, which I thought was a little odd as this was our first meeting. However, she was very comforting and settled my nerves immediately. I felt a positive connection with her as I began my one-on-one Reiki training and a two-year spiritual mentoring journey with this beautiful and knowledgeable soul.

We went downstairs to her nurturing retreat where she taught me all about Reiki, its history and how it works. Jacqueline shared with me how she discovered Reiki, which was both inspiring and emotional. I absolutely loved learning about energy and our ability to tap into this frequency of light and love at any time. After learning the theory, it was time for me to receive my first attunement to Reiki. An attunement is a sacred and spiritual practice that connects the recipient to and through the lineage of Reiki masters, and which allows the recipient to connect to the Universal Reiki energy.

The attunement was similar to my first experience of Reiki, only the feelings were greatly amplified. At the end of the session, Jacqueline asked me how my experience was. I couldn't find the words to describe how I felt because I was feeling so blissed out. I had a big smile on my face, for I knew then that I had been awakened to the most beautiful, loving and nurturing energy. It was a deeply sacred experience, felt with all my senses. It felt like coming home. I was invited into the energy and vibration of pure unconditional love, light and connection; it was an awakening for me to learn that I was also basking in the light of my own illuminated soul. The Reiki attunement allowed me to experience myself for the first time as a broader, more expansive being. While receiving the Reiki attunement, I felt enormous power which gently guided me into a place of pure stillness. It was in that moment I discovered who I truly was in my purest form, and embarked on this most fulfilling journey, learning how to live more of my life through this broader perspective.

Imagine coming face to face with your own soul and knowing in an instant that you are unconditionally loved - that you have never been alone and will never be. Reiki opened the door to a spiritual world that had, for many years, been just beyond my comprehension. My first glimpse into that world gave me a feeling of immense love, and made me very curious to learn more about myself, my soul and who was beyond the veil to support me.

Jacqueline later went on to teach me the standard hand positions for giving Reiki to yourself and others. I was also given the opportunity to practice Reiki on her. I remember feeling quite nervous the first time I gave her Reiki. Jacqueline reassured me, and it didn't take long before my nerves disappeared and were replaced with curiosity and a feeling of fun, especially when I felt the heat and Reiki energy gently surging through my body and hands.

I completed Reiki 1 and Reiki 2 in three short months, learning everything I could about energy healing and the world of spirit. I also had monthly spiritual mentoring sessions with Jacqueline, and embarked on a deeply personal healing journey that changed my life on every level. Of significance, I discovered that I was my own worst critic, lacking self-love and self-respect. Although I was often told that I was beautiful, talented and smart, those compliments really didn't get through the negative perceptions of myself. I was the greatest friend to others, and cared deeply about everyone else, but I never thought to share some of that love with myself. Jacqueline helped me to realise that I was perfect just the way I was.

I had always enjoyed smoking, but over time, I began to feel ashamed of being a smoker, and it showed. On several occasions while working at the hospital, I used to take a few minutes break from being Captain Starlight. During those breaks, I'd wear a jumper to cover up my uniform, and make my way to a little area on the border of the hospital grounds, which was surrounded by a garden, to hide and have a smoke. One day while puffing on my cigarette, I was confronted by the hospital chaplain who had followed the smell of smoke. She was very surprised, not to mention disgusted, to discover me sitting there with a cigarette in my hand. Although we had previously enjoyed a good relationship, it all changed in that moment.

What followed was a rather lengthy, very angry lecture. The chaplain told me that I should be ashamed of myself for smoking on the hospital grounds. She accused me of being insensitive to those who were in the hospital, and for not taking my role as Captain Starlight seriously. She said she never wanted to see me smoking on the hospital grounds again, and that if I was going to smoke, I should do so far off the premises where none of the children at the hospital could see me. This incident created within me such deep feelings of shame and humiliation; no one was more disappointed in myself than me. However, I continued to smoke.

Little did I know that smoking was my way of punishing myself for the guilt I felt.

I also recall another incident which highlighted my addiction to cigarettes and the shame associated with smoking. I was with a friend at an all-day Melbourne Cup horse racing event. It was a particularly hot day, and my friend and I had run out of cigarettes. So, we proceeded to line up at the cigarette dispensing machine with about twenty others who were in the same predicament. After waiting in line for about an hour in the heat of the sun, we arrived at the cigarette dispensing machine only to discover that all cigarettes were sold out. In a state of desperation, my friend and I began walking up to total strangers, asking them for cigarettes. The feeling of desperation was growing. After several angry rejections, one person finally gave us each a cigarette. With cigarette finally in hand, I recall feeling quite satisfied, but that feeling of satisfaction lasted about thirty seconds as what followed was a self-berating experience. I was disgusted by my behaviour, and, at that point, I found myself at a new low. Cigarettes were controlling my life, and I didn't like it one bit. I felt trapped by my addiction, and I couldn't find my way out.

During one of my sessions with Jacqueline, I told her that I smoked and found it very hard to quit. In response, Jacqueline presented me with a choice, something I had never considered. After hearing me talk about how much I loved Reiki, she gently gave me an ultimatum: "Do you want to be a smoker, Lisa, or a healer?"

The answer came immediately. "A healer."

Jacqueline went on to explain that healing starts with loving and nurturing myself and my body. Smoking demonstrated to the Universe that I didn't love myself or my body. That day, I was gifted with a totally new focus, one I had never considered before. On that day, I made the decision, quite simply, to be a healer and not a smoker. Why would I want to smoke when I can practice Reiki? Surprisingly, I didn't experience the common withdrawal symptoms which follow a nicotine addiction, because I had filled the space with something new that would help me to help others. My strong desire to help others through Reiki provided me with a new perspective on life. In that moment, I loved everything that Reiki and healing represented. I didn't really think much about smoking after that day as I had much to learn about Reiki and energy healing.

After I stopped smoking, it didn't take long before I started to look at many aspects of my life, including my desire to be an actor. After some soul searching, I came to realise that my passion and, at times, desperation to be a famous actor was just an excuse or means to avoid looking at myself. In a sense, acting gave me the freedom to be the person who I wished I could be through the roles and the characters that I would play.

Wanting to be more authentic in my life, I decided to focus on getting to know myself, which would mean putting down all the masks I had been hiding behind. My role of Captain Starlight was also one of them. A few years later, I left Starlight and the world of acting completely. I closed the door, quietly exited stage left, and walked down a brand new and exciting path of becoming a healer, Reiki Master, and the teacher that I am today.

WHAT IS REIKI?

History & Background

Reiki, a spiritual healing art, was founded by Mikao Usui in Japan in the 1920's. The term "Reiki" comes from two Japanese words, "Rei," meaning Universal Life, and "Ki," meaning Energy. According to the International Association of Reiki Professionals (IARP), Reiki is not affiliated with any particular religion or religious practice and is not based on belief or suggestion. Instead, it is a subtle and effective form of energy work that uses spiritually guided life force energy.

Reiki practitioners believe that this healing energy flows through all living things, and that everyone can connect with their own healing energy to strengthen themselves and others. When a person's Ki flows strong and free, their body and mind are in a positive state of health. However, when energy is weak or blocked, it can lead to physical or emotional imbalance.

Reiki was a popular practice in Japan before World War II, but it was later outlawed as a touch treatment after the war, which resulted in a significant decline in its popularity. As a result, Usui Reiki had to operate covertly for many years. Despite the challenges, Usui decided not to formalise Reiki as a religion, as he wanted it to be accessible to all individuals, a vision that remains unchanged to this day.

The Practice of Reiki

Reiki is a hands-on healing modality that involves channelling universal life energy or spiritual energy through the Reiki practitioner to the recipient. The experience of Reiki is unique to each practitioner, but it is common for the energy to enter through the crown chakra at the top of the head. The energy then flows down to the lower abdomen or belly, known as the "hara" in Japanese, and out through the practitioner's palms to the person receiving the treatment.

During a Reiki session, the energy flows through the body in response to the recipient's demand or need, allowing both the practitioner and recipient to receive the healing energy. Reiki intuitively goes to the root cause of a problem or situation, treating not only the symptoms but also the underlying cause of the imbalance. It enhances the body's natural healing ability and promotes overall wellbeing, making it a versatile healing practice.

Reiki is non-invasive and can be safely used to support traditional and complementary medicine. It does not interfere with other health or medical practices and can help ease tension and stress. A Reiki session is a relaxing and pleasant experience, often utilised for personal wellness and facilitating an environment for healing on all levels - physical, mental, and emotional.

Integration of Reiki into Healthcare

Reiki has gained popularity worldwide and is now practiced in various settings, including private practices, hospitals, nursing homes, and cancer support clinics. Patients have reported significant improvements in their level of pain, fatigue, nausea, and breathing, highlighting the benefits of using Reiki as a supportive healing practice. Its non-invasive and gentle nature makes it accessible to people of all ages and health conditions. As a result, it has become a widely used healing practice that helps individuals in different ways, promoting their physical, mental, and emotional well-being.

Intuitive Knowing & the Ego

"Intuition is the ability to know something without analytic reasoning, bridging the gap between the conscious and non-conscious parts of our mind".[1]

Intuition is a natural ability that we are all born with, but which many of us have forgotten how to use or trust.

---

[1] Mysoor A. (2017 February 2). The Science Behind Intuition and How you can use it to get Ahead at Work. *Forbes Women*. https://www.forbes.com/sites/alexandramysoor/2017/02/02/the-science-behind-intuition-and-how-you-can-use-it-to-get-ahead-at-work/?sh=39b8877b239f

Intuition is our internal place of inner knowing and our refuge from the outside world.

The most common question that I'm asked when I teach my classes is, "Are we all intuitive?" Yes, we are all born with a highly evolved, intuitive genius within. However, as we move into adulthood, we lose touch with this innate nature such that when we do get messages and guidance, we often dismiss them as fragments of our imagination. In fact, most people operate predominantly with their logical, rational mind and tend to ignore or suppress their emotions or their inner knowing. They identify themselves through their minds, beliefs and personality, which we call the ego.

The ego is the part of the mind that mediates between the conscious and the unconscious. It is responsible for reality testing and provides a sense of personal identity. It also makes up a person's sense of self-esteem or self-importance. In metaphysics, it is a conscious thinking subject.

I'm sure you've heard of people being referred to as "headstrong." While these people operate largely from their ego or masculine nature, others operate from their heart which reflects their feminine/intuitive nature. I have found that finding a balance between these two aspects of self is extremely important to clearly access my intuition, which in turn, helps me go through life with much more ease and grace. When we see life through the perception of the ego (sometimes referred to as the small "I am"), then we believe we are separate from God consciousness and each other. Not surprisingly, a great acronym for ego is "Edging God Out". In contrast, when we are in touch with our intuition, we are in tune with our higher power, also known as the big "I Am". Learning and practising Reiki strengthens your connection to your intuition, your higher power, your "I Am".

Having said that, the ego has a place in our human consciousness, innately keeping us safe. However, it also has the capacity to produce fear-based/negative thoughts that do not serve our highest good. We can find true peace when the mind or ego surrenders to the throne of the heart, for your heart has the capacity to hold you through all your negative emotions and love you unconditionally; this is Source working through you.

We can all access our divine self or this inner awareness. All that is needed is a little curiosity and a step-by-step approach that learning Reiki can provide.

What is Intuitive Reiki

Reiki is described by Mikao Usui in his manual, "The Usui Reiki Ryoho Gakkai" as *being intuitive.* When you learn Intuitive Reiki, you are given instruction on how to run Reiki energy, while at the same time, tune into your inner guidance/intuition, giving you greater clarity and confidence in your life. Intuitive Reiki practitioners, in contrast to traditional Reiki practitioners, have been trained to quiet their mind and connect with their clients energetically and spiritually. Through the process of giving and activating Reiki, the practitioners enter a trance-like state which allows them to experience the energy from both the recipient and the Universe, and to begin the journey of interpreting subtle messages they may receive. When Intuitive Reiki practitioners are in this open and receptive state, their senses are heightened, which allows them to read, know and understand the messages which filter in. The information is filtered through their heart, consciousness, mind and gut. When appropriate, and if the recipient is open to receiving in this way, the Reiki practitioner will then pass on the messages they have received. Messages received in this manner are supportive, kind, nurturing and encouraging.

Here is how I describe Intuitive Reiki to my students:

> *"Intuitive Reiki is when we are in an open and receptive state and we begin to see the world and our clients through the eyes of Source. We intuitively develop compassion not only for others, but also for ourselves, leading to greater self-love and healing on all levels."*

Through Reiki your ego takes a step back and the opening of your heart takes centre stage. You begin to see yourself and others through a higher and broader perspective; you have an awareness of yourself as a divine presence that is without form. Through Reiki, your spiritual heart opens and your connection to the divine and your intuition strengthens.

Principles of Reiki

At the very heart of the Reiki system are five guiding principles. Usui taught that when you make the decision to practise Reiki and to live by these principles, you are better able to live in balance, find alignment and happiness. The principles are:

> Just for today…
> I will not worry
> I will not anger
> I will be grateful
> I will do my work honestly
> I will be kind to every living thing

Practising the principles of Reiki and the energy it exudes will awaken your connection to spirit, and also help you to open and live from your heart; to assist you to deeply connect with yourself and others. Through Reiki you embark on a journey of self-healing by first recognising and then releasing the thoughts, beliefs and behaviours that no longer positively serve you. It is a journey of self-transformation, which occurs from a place of love. The more open and heart-centred you become, the easier it is to make positive changes in your life. Reiki also allows you to quiet the mind, thereby creating space for you to hear the inner whisperings of your heart and to access your higher power.

Practising the Reiki principles daily has helped me though my greatest challenges and provided me with hope and a positive framework to see me through.

Just for Today

"Just for today" is a reminder to be in the present moment as much as you can. I like to think of it as a gentle reminder that if we are living life through the confines of our mind, either hanging onto the past or worrying about the future, we can miss out on so much beauty that exists in life, here and now. For instance, I'm sure you've had the experience in which you were so focused on the chatter of your thoughts that you failed to notice the world around you; your attention and focus were directed through the lens of your concerns.

In contrast, when you apply the intention behind the phrase "just for today" you are more likely to redirect your attention to the present moment. Take nature for example. Have you ever gone for a walk and noticed all the beauty that surrounds you? The sensory experience of the way the wind touches your skin, or finding a place to sit and bask in the warmth of the sun as it radiates upon you? Or how about hearing the birds and being present with the beauty of their song, or looking up at the sky only to be reminded of how vast and expansive life is? According to Usui, when we are present, we are better able to access our soul's infinite wisdom, which leads us to make better and more fulfilling choices in our lives.

Just for Today, Do Not Worry

Many, if not all of us, worry. Worry causes us to feel anxious about actual or potential outcomes in the future. I believe at the core of this principle is the choice to live in fear or in love. Love is your natural state of being, but many of us operate from a place of fear, which stems from our life experiences and beliefs (many of them false and limiting) acquired over time. Whilst fear-based thoughts are products of the ego and intended to keep us safe, there are instances when acting out of fear or worry lowers your vibration and is disempowering. Reiki maintains that when you release the worry, you are more likely to live in the present. Better decisions are made and life tends to flow for the highest good for you and all concerned.

For instance, I have a friend who was running behind schedule and was worried about being late for a meeting. She was on the road during the early morning rush hour, and was stuck in traffic. Moving at a snail's pace, her worrying intensified. So, she decided to take an alternative route. In her haste to get to her destination on time, she began to drive over the speed limit. Unfortunately, she was pulled over for speeding, which caused her to be even later for the meeting.

How many times have you worried about a situation that never actually eventuated? Plenty, I'm sure. What a waste of precious and valuable time. Times which took you away from being and living in the present.

I was a chronic worrier. I worried about everything even when there was no reason to worry. In fact, my mother used to tell me that I worried about worrying, and I was once told that being a worrier was a part of my personality. I had difficulty making decisions, big and small, for fear that my decision would not be the right one. There were periods of time when my worry and anxiety became so acute, it was debilitating. I later realised that worrying was a behaviour that could be changed. When I began my Reiki journey, I quickly learned that I am solely responsible for my thoughts and feelings and that I am the only person who can change them. By implementing this principle, I became acutely aware of, and released my worrying thoughts. I began to worry less and began to make decisions from a trusting and empowered place. This practice gave me a strong sense of faith.

Just for Today, Do Not Anger

All of us experience anger from time to time. Anger is not necessarily a negative emotion. Rather, it is a sign that a person or an event has, perhaps, crossed a boundary. It's an emotion which is triggered by an external event or circumstance, and we often blame that particular event or circumstance for the anger.

However, according to Usui, anger is a reflection of what already exists within us and provides us with the opportunity to look beneath the anger. It provides us with the opportunity to question why such an event or circumstance has triggered the anger. In doing so, we learn to come to terms with the emotion and we begin to unravel the tapestry of life events that underpin the angry emotions. We discover what is commonly referred to as the shadow self; aspects of ourselves which need to be accepted and healed. When we're in anger, we are not seeing the event or circumstance objectively for what it truly is. In addition, responding angrily to a situation often makes matters worse.

For instance, I had a client, let's call her Paige, who used to get into a rage when her children would misbehave or disobey her. The anger was so disproportionate to the event that triggered her anger to the extent it bordered on being emotionally abusive to the children. After undergoing several Reiki sessions, Paige discovered that the anger she held was a result of her upbringing. Her mother was often emotionally and physically abusive to her whenever she failed to behave in a manner expected by her mother. Although Paige eventually blocked out those childhood memories from her conscious mind, she harboured huge resentment and anger, which she directed toward her children. Through Reiki, Paige recognised, accepted and eventually released the resentment and anger. Her perspective of her children's behaviour changed and she was no longer triggered by what she previously viewed as disobedient. Instead, she was calm, changing the manner in which she interacted with her children. As a result, communication between her and her family improved.

The energy of Reiki brings insight, understanding, and, most importantly, love and acceptance to our life's most painful memories and experiences we have endured. I have not met one person who hasn't been affected by guilt, shame, anger and pain. Many hold onto these feelings and, as a consequence, build emotional barriers to protect themselves – their hearts – from further pain. Although those barriers keep them safe to a degree, they also keep out the love that they are craving and deserve. To live by the principle, "do not anger," you embark on a journey of self-discovery and understanding of who you truly are.

Just for Today, Be Grateful

Gratitude is the antidote to worry and anger. Quite simply, it is impossible to have emotions of anger and worry when you are in gratitude. In addition, Usui explains, while worry and anger can cause illness in mind, body and spirit, the constant practice of gratitude can contribute to healing such illnesses. When you are in a state of worry or anger, practise gratitude on a daily basis, and focus your mind on all the people, places and things that make your life brighter or that bring you joy. Then your life will start to change for the better. You begin to vibrate at a higher frequency, which allows you to experience and exude more positivity in your life.

I recommend that you purchase a gratitude diary and make it a daily practice to jot down a few things that you are grateful for. If you do this as one of your morning rituals, your day will begin armed with a positive vibe. When you move through your day with appreciation, you'll find that your energy will pave the way for more things to appreciate throughout your day.

Just for Today, Do Your Work Honestly

This principle reminds us to work from a place of honesty and integrity towards others as well as yourself. It is akin to the "Golden Rule" of Leviticus 19:18 "Do unto others as you would have them do unto you." It is also a reminder for you to reflect upon your values and whether they serve your highest good as well as the highest good of others. We often inherit our parents' values, but as we go through life, those values may change to reflect what is most important to us and how we would like to live our life. It has been my experience that when you live by your personal values and this Reiki principle, life seems to unfold seamlessly for the good of all concerned.

I had a client who had just been told her young son had a brain tumour. She asked me if Reiki could heal her son and reduce his tumour. I believe in the human body's ability to heal itself and for Reiki to assist in that healing. Although I've always been open to the healing potential that Reiki offers, I was mindful not to promise healing or to give my client a false sense of hope, especially if it would influence her decision to seek further medical treatment for her son.

After the session I had a sense that my client was disappointed, because I didn't tell her what I suspect she desperately wanted to hear – that Reiki could heal her son. However, in my heart, I know I did the right thing by her as well as myself. I acted in alignment with what I felt was the best I could do. I could have appeased her by telling her what I suspected she wanted to hear, but I would not have been honouring the principle of Reiki, which in turn, would not have served her highest good in the long run. More importantly, it was not my intention to place my client in a position to choose between Reiki and western medicine. It's important to note that Reiki should always be considered as a complementary therapy and not as an alternative.

My intention is to provide my clients with a positive experience with Reiki. However, I can't control how others feel or how they may interpret the messages and guidance that comes through. I can only do my best and hope that it is enough. When all else fails, I turn back to the simplicity of Reiki and the love that it imparts.

Finally, I recall a conversation with a haematologist who told me about one of his patients who had an aggressive form of cancer and who had refused chemotherapy. His patient was religious, and based on his minister's counsel that his faith would heal him, he chose not to have chemotherapy. Consequently, his cancer progressed. He developed painful lesions all over his body and eventually became blind. The doctor told me that his patient suffered unnecessarily and believed that chemotherapy would have given him a better chance of slowing the progress of his cancer.

This story clearly demonstrates the importance of acting and living within a place of integrity, especially when practising Reiki. Although it was not the intention of the minister to cause unnecessary suffering to this man, it begs the question whether the minister's advice served the man's highest good. Did the minister consider the impact his words would have on this man's life? These are the types of questions we are asked to consider under the principle, "Just for today, do your work honestly."

Just for Today, Show Compassion and Loving Kindness

Practising compassion and kindness provides you the opportunity to see people and situations without judgement and anger. This principle asks you to change your perspective regarding a person or situation with which you may not quite agree or which doesn't fit nicely in your world or reality. At the core, this precept implores you to open your spiritual heart, and to accept and see the person or the situation before you from a higher perspective and through the eyes of love and compassion.

Attunements and Symbols

An attunement is a sacred and spiritual practice applied to students during the course of study of Reiki. In general, the study of Reiki is divided into three levels and includes a total of six attunements. These attunements are administered by Reiki Masters and serve to raise the vibration of the student and to strengthen the student's connection to their soul or higher self. The attunements also connect the student to the Reiki energy, their respective Reiki Master, as well as to the founder of Reiki, Mikao Usui and those masters who have followed in his lineage. At Reiki Level 1, four attunements are first introduced and applied as follows:

The first attunement serves to establish a connection between the student and the Reiki energy. This has the effect of increasing the student's energy and raising their vibration which, in turn, increases the student's ability to access Reiki's healing energy. The attunement opens the crown chakra, allowing the Universal Life Force Energy and wisdom to flow.

The second attunement allows the Reiki energy to operate through the student's etheric body or aura, which enhances the student's ability to connect with the spiritual realm. The attunement opens the neck and spinal region to improve the functioning of the nervous system and opens the throat chakra to enhance communication.

The third attunement serves to balance the student's right and left brain for clearer thinking and action.

The fourth attunement helps to clear the pituitary and pineal glands, allowing for an increase in consciousness and intuition. While the pituitary gland, located in the sixth chakra, (third eye) is understood to help balance the endocrine system, as well as the brain, the pineal gland located at the seventh chakra (crown), has the ability to perceive light and to connect one to Universal source energy.

This initiation completes the process allowing the

energy channels of the student to remain open. As such, once Reiki Level 1 has been completed, the student can run Reiki energy at a basic level, albeit not as a certified Reiki practitioner.

Reiki Level 2 introduces the student to the sacred Usui Reiki symbols and their use in the practice of Reiki. The symbols do not represent separate aspects of the Reiki energy, but rather are tools used to focus on different issues of the recipient. The symbols also help the practitioner perceive how the energy of Reiki is flowing through to the recipient. For example, there is a power symbol, a symbol to address mental and emotional issues, and a symbol to apply during distant healing sessions. There are also other non-traditional symbols which help to ground and clear energy, as well as symbols to apply as a Reiki Master practitioner.

Once the student has familiarised themself with the symbols, the symbols are energetically activated within the student through similar attunements as those introduced in Reiki Level 1. These activations enable the student to use the symbols for self-healing as well as to assist others in their healing process. Completion of Reiki Level 2 provides the student with the certification to practise Reiki in the public domain.

Many of my students report feeling an increase in the intensity of the Reiki energy during Reiki Level 2 sessions. I believe this increase in intensity is more likely due to the increased awareness in consciousness of those students since they were first introduced to Reiki. In my experience, working with the symbols can enhance one's spiritual experience by allowing the practitioner to channel Reiki intuitively, rather than from a logical point of reference.

In fact, many of my students state that their psychic senses are heightened.

The last level of Reiki is that of a Master. At this level the Reiki practitioner is given the Reiki Master symbol and is taught how to attune others as well as to be a teacher of Reiki. More significantly, once a practitioner has acquired this level of achievement, the intensity of their Reiki treatments may be amplified.

Although I teach the symbols traditionally used in Usui Reiki, the attunements and the methodology I apply are slightly different and are based on spiritual guidance I received during my early years of attuning small groups of people. I have always worked with a beautiful team of benevolent healing and teaching guides who have led me to make small changes over time regarding the way my students are initiated into Reiki.

Holding Space

Although not a basic Reiki tenet, during my Reiki classes I often speak about the power of "holding space" for others when we are giving them Reiki. This means that when channelling Reiki, you quiet your mind and become fully present to listen to and be with the recipient, and to offer unconditional love and support. Some of the most profound healing moments I have experienced have come through the quiet moments in which I hold space for my clients while they gently release their pain and emotion.

Reiki provides the perfect platform for you to hold space for another. It can guide you to be in pure alignment with love, and to build deep and profound compassion for another. Reiki not only allows precious time to slow down; it also raises your vibration/frequency to filter any messages you may receive.

Learning Reiki has given me an ability to see and live life from a very different perspective. And when I think of Reiki, I often reflect on the five Reiki principles and how they played a significant role in guiding me through one of the most challenging and life changing experiences.

Soul Mates & Living the Principles

I met Gerald when I was working at Starlight. Our first date was on Valentine's Day and we had what you would call a whirlwind romance. It didn't take long before I knew that he was the man my heart had been calling into my life. We had a strong, instant connection; it was as if, when I met him, my soul recognised him. He was different to the other guys I'd dated and our relationship felt very easy and comfortable. He was a deep thinker like me and so conversations with him were meaningful. Being with him made me so happy.

Nine months later, Gerald proposed to me. I remember the day as if it were yesterday. We were invited to attend a birthday party which was being held in a venue near the beach. The dress attire for the birthday party was formal, so Gerald, making the most of the occasion, hired a limo to take us to the party. When the limo picked me up, Barry White was playing and I thought to myself, *this is so bad, this couldn't possibly be when Gerald would be proposing to me.* However, my suspicions quickly dissipated as we started driving in the opposite direction of the party to a car park located below a scenic lookout to the ocean. That's when I knew what was happening. The wind was howling as I got out of the car, and the sun was setting, illuminating the horizon with a golden glow. Gerald took my hand and quickly led me up to the scenic landing on top of the hill. All I could think of was how embarrassing this was as we were both in formal attire and yet, at the same time, I was filled with joy and excitement. It wasn't until Gerald got down on one knee, took my hands in his and with the most incredibly well-prepared speech, explained to me why he had brought me to the lookout.

Our first date had been at the beach below the lookout. From where we stood, we had views of the sandy beach where it had taken place, and of the entire ocean of possibility laid out before us. He popped the question and presented me with the most exquisite ring, which to be honest, I had chosen with him many months before. We had discussed our desire to marry, but Gerald didn't feel comfortable choosing my wedding ring. He wanted to ensure that I had a ring that I loved, since I was to wear it for the rest of my life. So one Saturday afternoon, we went to the jewellery store together to look for a ring of my choice. When I finally found the ring of my dreams, he said that he needed to pay it off before he could propose to me. So, although I knew Gerald would be my life partner, I had no idea how and when he would ask for my hand in marriage. Boy, was I caught by surprise. Obviously, my answer was "yes."

We were married nine months later in September 2004. We travelled across the world to Hawaii for our honeymoon, and when we returned home, we purchased our first house together. Shortly after returning from Hawaii, I fell pregnant with our beautiful daughter, Georgia.

Getting married was a dream come true, and becoming a mother was a deeply profound experience. Nearly two years after Georgia's birth, I fell pregnant again. We were elated, but when I was three months pregnant with our second child, Hannah, I received a call that would change the course of our life.

Our Happiness Bubble Burst

After having Georgia, I left Starlight and was working part time at the ANZ bank as a teller when my boss told me that I had an urgent phone call. Gerald had been unwell for about a week with what we thought at the time was a bad cold. He went to the doctor who gave him a thorough examination and ran blood tests. When the test results came back, they indicated that Gerald's immune system was not functioning properly, if at all. As a result, Gerald was told that he needed to go to hospital right away. I immediately called my mum and dad, and Gerald's parents, Reg and Stella, to relay the devastating news. I then called my best friend, Kristen, and explained through a flood of tears what was happening, and that I was worried Gerald could have leukaemia. Kristen gently said, "That's the worst-case scenario. Let's just wait and see what the doctors say before you get too worried."

Unfortunately, it didn't take long before the doctor confirmed my fears. Of all places we were sitting in a children's room at the hospital, as the emergency ward was full.

Although we were in a private room, it didn't especially reflect the way I was feeling; it was painted bright yellow with cartoon characters all over the walls. After what seemed like an eternity, the doctor came in and told us that Gerald had an acute form of Leukemia, Acute Myeloid Leukaemia (which was the same type of Leukemia that Brittany had died of), and that he was to start treatment immediately.

For me, being in a children's room took me right back to my Starlight days in the children's hospital. All the experiences that I had at Starlight came flooding back to me, including fear. I kept my fearful emotions to myself as I didn't want to scare Gerald. He, on the other hand, was quite relaxed about the whole thing; while I wondered whether the leukemia would prematurely end his life, he asked if this was something that he would have to manage for the rest of his life. He kept making jokes to the point that the nurse on duty pulled me aside and asked me if he understood the seriousness of the diagnosis he had just been given. I had no idea what Gerald was thinking, but it may have just been his way of coping. Or perhaps he was in denial, because he felt perfectly fine within himself at the time. He didn't start to feel sick until a few weeks later when the medical treatment took hold.

Those first few weeks were a total blur. I was three months pregnant and having a hard time coping with the stress. Consequently, on the advice of my doctor, I began to take anti-depressants, based on the assurance they would not harm our unborn baby. Gerald spent six months in and out of isolation in hospital. During his time in hospital, he was given three rounds of aggressive chemotherapy, had a central line inserted just short of his heart, and had a myriad of tests conducted which were too many to remember.

We spent many moments crying and holding each other, and with each moment I spent with him, I could feel the Reiki flow. Then one day I had an experience that took me by surprise. I remember it as though it happened yesterday. I was sitting at the end of the bed in Gerald's room. He was recovering from the second round of chemotherapy and was extremely weak. I looked over and saw him standing in the shower - totally vulnerable. The strong man that I had met and knew from a few years before, now looked so very week and frail. Suddenly, I felt this feeling of profound love move through me like a wave. On reflection, it began as a feeling of sadness and then changed to a feeling of deep love. I realised how important this man was in my life and, in that moment, I loved him more than I can put into words. I felt so very sad for the pain he was enduring. It was like my heart broke. I also felt such fear that this disease might take my beloved from me. However, that empathy, fear and grief moved into a feeling of such powerful love. It was as if I had been given a choice to see him from fear or to realise how much I deeply loved him. Luckily for the both of us, I chose love. I chose to release the worry, judgement and any anger I held regarding the situation, and in doing so, in that moment, I realised how very fortunate I was and grateful to have him in my life.

After several minutes, he came out of the shower and asked me if I was okay. I have no idea what expression I wore, but I just took his great big, beautiful face and gave him a kiss, and simply told him that I loved him. Gerald was given the "all clear" two days before Hannah was born in 2008, marking the beginning of a new chapter in our life.

After reflecting on this difficult, but life changing experience, I've come to realise that Reiki and implementing its precepts daily played an integral part in Gerald's healing process. Gradually, the worry and anger we felt from time to time were replaced by focusing on the positives in our lives; we decided that every day we would find something to be grateful for, from the simple gift of a cup of tea to a smile from the hospital staff. While Gerald chose to use western medicine, we saw this as only one small part of his healing. The practice of Reiki provided us with the belief and trust that the body could heal itself. Gerald had many moments to contemplate his life and he really did surrender to his higher self. He told me that he was going to trust the doctors to take care of his physical body as he recognised that he was not just his body. He surrendered to accept the situation and knew that dying was not an option for him. He recognised that he was the sum total of all the choices he had made and reflected on the choices that may have played a part in him becoming sick.

One of the positive things about being in hospital for long periods of time was that Gerald also had plenty of time to think about his own happiness. He did a life review of sorts and discovered that there was one part of his life where he felt unhappy. He realised that his work wasn't aligned to his natural talents and abilities, and that he chose to become a sales representative, not because he loved sales, but because the role could provide him with financial gains and prestige. So, while in hospital, he decided to work out what he might love to do instead. After reflecting on his life and the things he used to love doing as a child and into his early twenties, Gerald realised that one of his fondest, most joyful memories was when he designed and renovated his first home with his father. As a result, after Gerald completed his medical treatment, he studied to become a draftsperson. Soon after graduating, he left his job as a sales representative, and was given a position at a very well-established building company, where he is still working and loving it.

Gerald and I believe that his reflection and understanding of his life, without judgement, was a result of the love that Reiki provides. My husband was clearly led to have more compassion and love for himself, which contributed to his recovery. (To note, we recently discovered that it is rare for someone to survive from this form of cancer.) Chaos came and delivered us right into love's embrace. The love and support of our family and friends, Reiki, as well as my husband's amazing ability to find the positive in any situation, has given us both a platform for profound growth and change. We often reflect on the gifts that have come from the adversity we have faced together during our marriage. One of the scariest moments in my life became one of the greatest catalysts for experiencing profound and deep love, which for me continues to this day.

When you follow the principles of Reiki and begin to apply them to the situations in your life, you begin to realise that you always have a choice. When I am confronted with a problem or a situation which triggers a negative emotional response in me, it usually means that a negative or limiting belief is being brought to my awareness. It is then that I can choose to either remain in such a state of worry or fear, or to accept and understand it, and ultimately change my perspective of the situation from a place of love and compassion.

For example, I recall in one of the sessions with my psychologist, Zoe, I was feeling extremely distressed and helpless to the point of hysteria regarding Gerald's illness. I expressed to Zoe my fear that Gerald was going to die. After unloading my emotions, Zoe looked me in the eye with a gentle but kind concern, and asked me where Gerald was. Surprised by her question, I stopped crying to process an answer and replied that he was in the hospital. "Can you call him?" she asked.

"Yes, I could if I wanted to."

She then asked if I spoke to him often while he was in hospital. I replied, "Every day. We even watch TV together like we would at home, once I've put Georgia to bed."

Zoe then said something that would profoundly change my life and pave the way to deal with Gerald's health challenges with more ease and grace. "Well then. Right now, Gerald is still alive and able to chat and spend quality time with you, both in person and over the phone. I want to let you know, Lisa, that no amount of preparation you could do now would make his passing any less difficult or painful. Would you agree?"

I thought about it for a moment and acknowledged that his death would totally devastate me. She went on to say, "He's still alive so how about we deal with his death if and when it happens? And let's also acknowledge right now that there is a huge possibility that it might not happen any time soon. Would you agree?"

In that moment, it became clear to me that I was wasting precious time worrying about whether Gerald would die, instead of celebrating his life with him. I was so worried about the future, which took me out of being in the present with Gerald, and being grateful that he was still alive. I had a shift of perspective from fear to love.

Gerald has been in remission since 2008, and, at the time of writing this book, hasn't had a relapse. He's also very healthy; he eats well, runs long distances five to six times a week, and has just completed his first ultra-marathon.

UNDERSTANDING EMOTIONS AND THOUGHTS

Emotions and Intuition

Did you know that your emotions are your internal guidance helping you to know if you are in tune with your intuition or not. The way you are feeling is a powerful indicator of whether the thoughts you're thinking are in alignment with what I refer to as *Source, the I Am, God* or *Goddess.*

Think about the last time you were really excited about something. It may have been a meeting you were going to or an encounter that you were about to have. Whatever the situation, that good feeling is our natural way of knowing that we are on the right path, tuned in to, and connected with what we really want, not what we think we should be doing, or worse still, what we think others think we should be doing. In contrast, your intuition also serves to warn us when we're "off track", or when something or someone is not in alignment with our highest good.

For instance, I had a client a few years ago who came to see me for a series of Reiki sessions. On the surface everything seemed fine and nothing about the client appeared out of the ordinary. However, during each session, I felt increasingly uneasy and uncomfortable. At the time, I didn't understand why I was feeling so uncomfortable with this client, but when I later reflected upon the experience, I realised there was a series of events that caused my uneasiness.

It all started at his first session. When he arrived at my centre, I asked him to take a seat, but he completely ignored me and continued to wander around the centre. As an isolated incident, his behaviour didn't cause me any concern. However, about five minutes into the first session, I asked him a question to which he didn't reply. I was confused as I was sure he heard me, so I asked again, and again he failed to reply. I continued with the session, thinking that, maybe, he fell asleep. But I was wrong. I eventually realised that he was awake and just didn't want to talk. During a session, it's important for me to engage with the client so that I can better understand what aspect of the client needs healing. Channelling Reiki in silence is not my usual protocol, and his unwillingness to converse piqued my curiosity and, at the same time, made me feel somewhat uncomfortable. To note, although there are periods of silence during my sessions, these interludes are peaceful and relaxing, and provide the client with a time of quiet reflection. This certainly was not the case. I felt uncomfortable, which was my intuition giving me a warning.

I treated him twice after that initial session, and at each visit he brought crystals and other paraphernalia which he wanted me to use during his sessions to see whether they would amplify the effects of Reiki. Although I occasionally work with crystals in my practice, I had no knowledge about the healing properties of his crystals. In addition, he told me where to place the crystals on his body, which made me feel uneasy. He even requested that I remove my shoes while I treated him. Even though this was not a common practise of mine, I reluctantly did so. At this point, I felt that he was in total control of the session, challenging the integrity of my practice, which left me feeling insecure and vulnerable. Finally, during his last session he placed his hands on top of mine when I was giving him Reiki over his hips, which has never happened with a client in all my years in practice. I quickly slid my hands out from under his and moved to his knees. I was left feeling extremely uncomfortable for the remainder of the session. After his session ended I decided I wouldn't work with this client again.

I don't know if this man had any intention of causing me personal harm and I'd like to think that he did not, but my intuition was telling me all along something wasn't quite right. This experience taught me that while I always like to see the best in others, I must trust and listen to my inner knowing – that still small voice within, as not all people are who or what they appear to be.

In addition, if our emotions are hidden, suppressed and ignored, we tend to rely more on our thoughts and our past experiences to guide us through our decision-making process. The ego, or our logical/rational mind, becomes the dominant factor and can be very fear-based in its decision-making capabilities. It stores and remembers vast amounts of experiences you've had in life, both good and bad, and will usually guide you to future decisions based on what you experienced in the past. It follows then, that if you haven't had the happiest of life experiences, you are more likely to be guided by limited, fear-based thoughts and emotions, and not be in alignment with your intuition/Source.

Sometimes our inner knowing can be drowned out by our desire to please others. This behaviour is especially acute and learned from early childhood when many of us are programmed to please our parents in order to obtain praise and/or love in return. As a result, many grow through life making choices for the sake of pleasing others as the right thing to do, only to ignore subtle indicators from their intuition that they are out of alignment with who they truly are. I believe that we can only access lasting inner happiness when we are living in alignment with our truest desires, rather than living life to placate the desires of others.

I met a woman who completed a degree in a subject that she wasn't especially interested in to please her father. She didn't like what she was learning, but persisted because she thought it was what she should do. Unhappiness ensued, and as a result, she spent another three years at university (six years in total) to finally get the degree in a subject that was of interest to her and which, in turn, brought her happiness. Many years were wasted, not to mention the cost of obtaining the degree she would never use, all to please her father. I believe that if she was tuned into her intuition, she wouldn't have continued to pursue that first degree.

You will experience a whole range of emotions during your lifetime, and rest assured, it is safe, if not, beneficial, to explore all your emotions, the good and the not so good ones. Reiki gives us the tools and the process to help us to discover what our truest desires are. It gives us access and insights to our own unique path of spiritual and personal fulfilment. Over the years, I have found that it is helpful for me to explore my negative emotions with openness and gentle curiosity; to seek to understand, rather than to avoid them, and to not let my emotions control me and my life. What I know for sure is that when we can be kind and gentle with ourselves and seek to understand why we feel a certain way, the energy moves swiftly through us, and we can get back to the present moment and to the truth of the situation at hand.

This poem is one I love, because it teaches us that all our emotions are messengers which, if we take heed of them, can guide us to living more authentic and fulfilled lives.

Your Body is a Guest House

Listen, oh beautiful soul.
Every day a new feast
comes running into your life.
Always a new experience.

Your body is like a guest house,
receiving company from the hidden world.
Some are positive,
some are tragic,
and still others who are frantic.

All mirroring your needs.
All showing you ways to expand.
All challenging your beliefs.

Whoever that comes from these unseen lands,
receive it without regret.
Welcome all that come to you,
with no judgement.

Remember, every visitor,
here a short time,
meant only for your growth.

—Rumi poem Your Body is a Guest House from the book *Rumi: The Beloved Is You*, by Shahram Shiva, is being used by the permission of Rumi Network.

Can you start to think of your emotions in this way, as welcome visitors to the open and loving home of your own divine and loving heart?

Being the Observer

Learning how to understand and manage my emotions has been an interesting journey for me as I naturally tend to filter my life experience through my emotions. Where others are more logical, I'm more emotional. I used to see life as a success when I felt happy. In contrast, when I was angry or sad, or feeling guilty or ashamed, I would begin to ruminate over negative thoughts and stories, which made me feel even worse. I learned that negative emotions do not represent who I truly am, and that I have a choice as to how I respond to life.

I remember being emotionally triggered during a coaching session with business coach, Marnie LeFevre. We were in a busy café and I became embarrassed when an emotion arose within me during our session. I started crying and then apologised for crying. Marnie asked me if I would apologise for laughing in a café, to which I said "no." She then pointed out that I didn't need to apologise for crying either, because all emotions are beautiful. Marnie gently guided me through a process that helped me to identify the issue which caused the emotion without shutting it down. Through accepting and embracing the emotion, the embarrassment I felt in that moment naturally subsided.

Later that day at home, I reflected upon what had occurred in the café. It was clear Marnie helped me to change my perspective of the situation. I was able to apply the principle, *just for today, do not worry*, and as a result, I was able to detach myself from those negative emotions, and observe them instead. By simply observing my emotions and behaviour without judgement, I was better able to accept, forgive and have more compassion for myself.

It is worth noting here that the Reiki principles do not suggest that we ignore our emotions; rather, the practice of Reiki provides an opportunity to see ourselves through a higher perspective – through the frequency of love – to uncover the basis of the negative thoughts and emotions which underpin our beliefs. Reiki is love, and when we align to love we begin to accept and honour all aspects of ourselves and others, and our world. I truly believe that there is only love, and when we can surrender to the love within us all, we find peace and contentment.

The practice of Reiki helps you to become the observer. In fact, viewing others and situations objectively is paramount to the effective practice of Reiki. By being a neutral observer, we can find the truth of a situation, and better understand ourselves and others. We can then move to a state of acceptance and compassion, bringing us back into balance and harmony once more. This doesn't mean that you're unattached to any emotions you may feel. Rather, being the observer means you're not getting emotionally engaged in the story or drama of another. It is having compassion without attachment to any outcome of a situation. More importantly, being the observer in Reiki forces you to be present and enhances your ability to intuitively connect with your recipient.

I recall I had a client in her early twenties. She was feeling stressed and anxious, and upon a friend's recommendation, she came to me for a Reiki session. During the session, I intuitively picked up a strong current of energy coming from her lower abdomen and channelled Reiki in the area for a longer period than usual. This energy is referred to as Byosen energy and has been described as the "frequency of 'sick accumulation' that is emitted from a tense, injured or ill part of the body... It is also the reaction of the body to incoming Reiki energy." [2]

As I continued to channel Reiki, I kept being drawn to my client's lower abdomen, intuitively sensing that she may have been experiencing some issues in this area. I gently checked with my client to see whether she was okay, being mindful that as a Reiki practitioner, it is not my place to medically diagnose clients. However, I trusted that the Reiki was doing what it does best, going naturally to the area of need and assisting the body to release any energy blockages. As a result, when I asked if she felt any pain in this area, she very nervously opened up and told me that she had an abortion, a part of her life which she hadn't shared with anyone. Once she released this long held secret, she was then able to share the guilt and shame she felt about her decision to abort. After discussing at length her feelings and the circumstances surrounding her decision, she came to realise that the only way for her to move past this painful and traumatic experience was through acceptance and self-forgiveness. Over a series of Reiki sessions with me, she gradually made peace with herself and her past. More

---

[2] Petter, A, F. (2007). Understanding Byosen Scanning, Part II. *International Centre for Reiki Training.*
https://www.reiki.org/articles/understanding-byosen-scanning-part-ii

significantly, she overcame the depression and anxiety from which she had suffered for years.

I cannot emphasise enough that one of the most important aspects of Reiki is to observe a situation or client without judgement; to put one's beliefs and opinions aside and come from a place of neutrality. To illustrate, throughout my life I have been against the use of recreational drugs and, as a result, formed strong negative opinions about those who engaged in this sort of activity. Then one day a woman, who was a recovering drug addict, came to see me for a Reiki session. During the session, she released a barrage of emotions that she had supressed for many years and shared that she used to be a heavy illicit drug user, which led her to do things she now painfully regrets doing. She went on to relay the trauma and pain she had endured and was still experiencing as a result of the choices she had made in the past. Before my Reiki journey, I would have formed a negative opinion about her. However, witnessing the obvious distress and sadness this woman was experiencing through the eyes of Reiki, I instead felt enormous love and compassion for her. Reiki not only provided her the freedom to share her story, but it provided me the space to understand and to respect this woman on a deeper level. Through Reiki, I have learnt to be less judgemental. I believe that unless I have walked in another's shoes, I can never truly know the intricacies of another's life, or why they make the choices that they make. Reiki guides us into compassion and offers us a unique and beautiful pathway to help ourselves and others.

Power of Your Mind

Learning Reiki is a great step towards helping people, but more importantly, Reiki is a pathway to self-awareness, self-development and self-love. Whilst training in Reiki, I came to understand the power our mind has over our experiences and I began to process the negative emotions and release the limiting beliefs or blocks that were holding me back in life. Reiki gave me a wonderful ability to move through any issues I was facing with ease and grace, rather than with judgement and shame. I learned early on in my training that understanding my emotions is paramount to integrate the Reiki principles into my life. It is also key in developing my intuition. I remember posting the Reiki principles on my bedroom wall and on the fridge, reminding myself daily of the way I wanted to live. I became very interested in why and how I was responding to life, and the role my mind plays in my overall happiness and healing. And so, when the time was right in my life, I decided to complete my diploma in Clinical Hypnotherapy and Psychotherapy. I then went on to complete a diploma in Neuro Linguistic Programming (NLP). As my Reiki skills developed, so too did my desire to obtain further training in helping others.

Through the study of hypnotherapy, I came to understand that the ego is, by default, primarily fear-based and intended to keep us safe. Although it plays a very important role in our life, it is also responsible for negative thoughts that sabotage us. In my hypnotherapy and NLP training, I learned a process called anchoring, which helps one to counteract those negative thoughts. It is a process in which we anchor or state positive suggestions to help reinforce positive changes that people would like to make in their life. For example, I chose to anchor the belief that life keeps getting better and better for me. Then, to give it greater impact, I anchor that belief when I am having fun and a positive experience. Over time, we start to become very intentional with our thoughts and life responds to us, bringing more of what we are wanting into our experience.

When you work with the Reiki principles, it can be helpful to find a way to anchor a new positive belief into your daily practice. For example, when you are having a shower, you could anchor the thought that when you turn the tap on, you will focus on the Reiki precept, *just for today*. Consequently, every time you have a shower you will be reminded to be fully present with the experience of washing your body and giving yourself Reiki while you are in the shower as a way of nurturing yourself and calming your mind.

Another example is while brushing your teeth in the morning, you could anchor the suggestion that just for today, you will be grateful, taking a moment to think about something or someone that you appreciate. Gratitude soon starts to become an attitude and a practice. Or before each meal, you could anchor the suggestion that just before you pick up your knife and fork to eat, you channel Reiki to your food by holding your hands above your plate while appreciating what it took for the food to be on your plate.

THE NEXT STEP

Answering the Call from Spirit

I recall a time when life would give me an experience that would teach me just how powerful my intuition is and how detrimental it can be when I don't follow its messages and impulses. It is one thing to interpret your intuition, but it's another to act on it, especially when doing so takes courage to stand up for what you believe is right. I was faced with a situation that created an opportunity for me to act and trust my intuition, or to ignore it completely to appease others. Unfortunately, I chose to ignore my intuition, and the results were devastating.

When my youngest daughter Hannah was eighteen months old, we went on a family holiday in Sydney. The holiday was at a stunning property owned by my husband Gerald's Uncle Les and Auntie Judy, and which was more remote than I would have liked. While Gerald has always loved nature and camping, I prefer a proper roof over my head with all the modern comforts of a 5-star retreat. Nevertheless, it was a beautiful drive through the Blue Mountains to reach Molong, which is about 300 kilometres from the city. As we were heading into the town, we drove past the local hospital. I was expecting the place we were staying at to be more remote, so seeing the hospital, for some reason, brought me a feeling of relief.

The property on which we stayed was stunning and quirky. There was a train carriage, which had been renovated to sleep eight guests, perched on top of a hill with incredible views across the valley. On the right-hand side of the train was a campfire that had seen many family gatherings, and lots of heart-felt sharing and laughing. There was no running water or electricity so, to Gerald's delight, we were having an off-the-grid experience.

It was bedtime for our daughters, Hannah and Georgia. The sun had set, teddies were unpacked, and beds made. While Gerald proceeded to read Georgia a story in the lounge/kitchen area, I began to prepare Hannah's bottle while chatting to Judy; I filled up a metal container with boiling water and placed her bottle into it to warm. Unbeknownst to us, Hannah walked over to the kitchen counter, reached up on her tippy toes and pulled down the bottle, spilling the full cup of boiling water all over her tiny body. Hannah screamed the kind of scream no mother wants to hear. That sound went right through me, a piercing and painful scream that didn't stop.

I quickly picked her up and started looking for a source of running water, but there was none. Off the grid meant there was only dam water available. While Judy drenched a towel with pure water from a large bottle, Les calmly asked Gerald to get the first aid book out of the drawer and read out the course of action. We took off Hannah's clothes to reveal the burn. It started at her left shoulder then ran all the way down her arm to her left hand. Her arm was bright red and she was in a lot of pain. With the soaking wet towel wrapped around her arm, Les drove Hannah and me to the hospital, which thankfully, was only five minutes down the road. Hannah screamed and tried to pull the wet towel off her arm the entire way there.

When we arrived at the hospital, she was quickly assessed by the local doctor. The nurse then used iced water to cool the burn. Intuitively, I knew in my gut it was the wrong thing to do. However, when I questioned the nurse, she said the doctor knows what he's doing and she was merely following his instructions. Against my own instincts, I did as I was told and held my little girl in my arms while they unwrapped the towels and then proceeded to wrap her arm with a wet towel filled with iced water. When it was applied to her arm, it was clear by her crying that her pain intensified, and so again, I questioned the process. Again, I was told to do as the doctor said. I continued to ignore my gut, my inner knowing, and allowed the doctor to treat my child in a way that I knew was not helping her, but in fact, was inflicting even more pain. I didn't listen to my intuition and my daughter paid the price, all for the sake to please a doctor I didn't even know and would likely never see again.

As soon as the doctor left the room, I started to think more clearly. It was at this point I remembered that I could turn to Reiki for help. I was lying on the hospital bed with

Hannah in my arms. I gently loosened the iced water towel and began to send Reiki healing to her arm with my hands hovering five centimetres above the area of the burn. As soon as I started to run the energy, she stopped crying and began to relax. I then put my hand on her little heart, and the comforting and nurturing Reiki energy continued to flow. Shortly thereafter, she fell asleep in my arms, exhausted but with some relief from her pain. Reiki eased her physical pain and helped her to relax, but it also comforted me at the same time. I went from a high state of anxiety and overwhelming helplessness to a calm and relaxed place of peace. Through Reiki, my baby was settled and I was feeling much better as well, but not for long.

We were transferred the next day to the main hospital in Sydney, where Hannah's burns were assessed and treated with a new silver dressing, which was proven to reduce the chance of infection and help assist the body's own natural healing process. We were told that she was very lucky not to have sustained the burns across her fingers or any of the joints on the inside of her arms. She had two second-degree burns which were rather large on her bicep and two slightly smaller ones on her lower arm. If the burns had been across the joints, Hannah would have required surgery as, given her young age, new skin growth over those areas would not have occurred. Hannah's burns missed all those main areas of concern, which was a huge relief to us. The doctor reviewed Hannah's medical notes and congratulated us on how well we had handled the burn when it first happened. He went on to tell us a few of the ways people first treat burns which, in fact, exacerbates the wound rather than helps. He explained that the best way to treat a burn when it first happens is with room temperature water and not iced water.

"Excuse me. What did you just say?" I asked as a feeling of dread started to wash over me. "Using ice to cool a burn actually further burns the child," he said.

Once I had processed what I had just been told, I instantly regretted that I had ignored my intuition and inner knowing, and allowed the first doctor to treat Hannah's burns with iced water. I told the doctor how Hannah was treated, and with a concerned look on his face, he gently said, "We haven't iced burns for many years." With a heavy heart, I thanked him, and we left with Hannah's arm bandaged from her wrist all the way to the underarm.

When we returned to the hotel and the children were asleep, a wave of mixed emotions rolled through my body and I began to sob. I cried over the pain that Hannah had endured, but at the same time, I felt so grateful that Hannah's burns were minor compared to the burns victims I saw while I worked at the children's hospital. Yet, more significantly, I felt such grief and guilt for not listening to my inner knowing, for had I done so, Hannah would have been less traumatised.

I cried myself to exhaustion and finally surrendered to accept what had transpired. At that point, a feeling of hope started to rise from deep within me – a calling. My experience with Hannah was a turning point for me. I promised I would do all I could to learn more about my intuition, to discover how to trust it, and most importantly, to learn how to have the courage to act on it.

The Transformative Power of Reiki

I began my Reiki practice in 2003. In those early days, I became aware of my intuition and was able to sense a presence around me. Not knowing how to handle this newfound awareness, my ego would often go into overdrive and dismiss my intuitive insights, replacing them with fear, doubt and insecurity. I continued to work with Jacqueline to help me understand and release my fear of the spiritual world. Learning from Jacqueline was a deeply transformative experience. While working at Starlight, Jacqueline helped me to view experiences and cases from a spiritual perspective. She also taught me some of the deeper principles of Reiki and how applying those principles in my life would lead to more inner peace and happiness.

During my Reiki sessions, I came to understand that I was highly intuitive, and that the presence I felt around me were spirits, angels and other light beings. I also began to hear messages, which meant nothing to me, but were significant and meaningful to the recipient. I came to realise that other Reiki practitioners were not having the same experience; many said that Reiki was just running energy. I then knew that I had always had an ability to perceive the spirit world. As a teenager, I recall seeing spirits and was extremely afraid of them. Although I didn't fully understand what my experiences meant, I chose not to explore and learn more about this phenomenon. As a result, my connection to spirit also stopped. It wasn't until I embarked on my Reiki journey that I began to realise that my connection with spirit experienced in my early teens was the same connection I was experiencing during a Reiki session, receiving intuitive insights and messages.

I became certified as a Usui Reiki Master in 2008, eight months after Hannah was born. During this period in my life, I met Rayeleen, the owner of a holistic healing practice which was called *Harmonious* and would later be re-branded to *Yes 2 Life*. I told Rayeleen I had recently become a Reiki Master, and she asked me if I would like to come and work at her centre, teaching Reiki classes as well as offering Reiki sessions to patrons. I was elated! I felt like it was a gift from the Universe and the perfect opportunity to leave my part-time job at the bank. A few months later, I taught my very first Reiki workshop. I was expecting four students and worked an entire weekend preparing for the workshop. However, when I arrived at the centre, I was met with six new students. I felt unprepared to teach six students, but I trusted that it was meant to be. Rayeleen also believed in me and told me that she knew I was ready for the challenge. And so I began, and the rest is history.

I'm still teaching group workshops and loving it. The energy created in the workshops is often transformative. More significant and rewarding are the friendships that are formed amongst the students and with me.

Awakening Psychic Abilities

While working at *Yes 2 Life* I met Samantha Duly, who is an International Spiritual and Psychic Medium, and who had a huge impact in my life. Samantha ran a development circle aimed at training and developing one's intuition and psychic/mediumship abilities. Over the next four years, I attended her development circle every week, learning to understand and connect to the subtle world of spirit. This practice is called psychic or spiritual mediumship in which mediums can sense and communicate with people who have passed away, and relay messages they receive to the bereaved.

As I started to learn more about spirit and develop my mediumship skills, I realised that when I was attuned to Reiki, my ability to communicate with the spirit world was amplified. Whilst I felt more comfortable in my mind separating the two modalities of Reiki and mediumship, putting them both into practice with my clients truly helped me to provide a more meaningful and impactful service to my clients. Gradually over time, messages started to flow with ease while I was giving Reiki to my clients. Suffice it to say, most of my clients were delighted to get a combined session of both Reiki and a reading.

However, about four years after I began working in this way, I began to question whether how I practised was appropriate; this was not the norm for most practitioners, and I wondered if I should continue working in this manner. As serendipity would have it, I was then introduced to Marnie, who would then help me to integrate the two modalities, and to feel comfortable doing so.

Because of my training in mediumship, I gained a beautiful outlook on the transition experience. My understanding of what happens when people make their transition from this world to the next has brought so much love, peace and healing to those who have suffered through the pain when someone they love dies. I will say that grief is a deeply personal experience and no two people experience grief in the same way. When I've lost friends and family members,

I have found that having a spiritual perspective has made processing and moving forward in life much easier. Helping others through their grief can be very fulfilling; to see people shift their perspective and receive answers from the spiritual world directly is also very rewarding and humbling work. If you are interested in communicating with spirit, I suggest that you learn under the guidance of an experienced and qualified teacher. However, as with all great achievements in life, dedication and practice are essential as there are no short cuts to becoming a great medium.

Introducing Intuitive Reiki International

When we first met, Marnie was the director of a large women's festival called *Secrets in the Garden*. Her presentation at the festival was about running a successful business. When she stepped onto the stage, one of the first things she said was, "I've been tuning into you from backstage while I was waiting to come out and speak…and you all have such beautiful energy." I was immediately intrigued by her initial address as I found it unusual for someone in the business world to mention energy. She seemed to be open to spirituality too. Her talk was engaging, and I was impressed by her humour and stage presence. I found myself really leaning in and wanting to learn more from her.

After her presentation, I waited in line to introduce myself. When I told her my name, she knew who I was and mentioned she wanted to learn Reiki. She added that she had been guided by her grandmother in spirit to learn from me. A little surprised and excited, we exchanged contact details and the following week she asked me if I would be open to a session swap - Reiki for a business coaching session. I was delighted as she charged about ten times the amount than I did back then!

Marnie came to the centre where I was working and I gave her Reiki. She was also open to receive any messages and/or guidance that came through. The session proceeded and I passed on many messages that came through for her. When the session was over, we then began a very inspiring business coaching session in which she gathered as much information about my current Reiki practice. I explained to Marnie that when I run Reiki energy, my mind is elevated to a place where I can see, hear and feel spirit clearly, and messages seem to flood through my being. What happens to me is an intuitive way of working with Reiki, and while it feels so natural to me, it is not the norm in the industry. Some Reiki schools don't believe in or allow their students to mention working with the spirit world. They believe that working with spirit is not Reiki. As a consequence, this instilled a sense of fear for being intuitive and for passing on messages I received during a Reiki session.

After our first coaching meeting, Marnie helped me to see the benefits of the way I work, and she wanted to support me in integrating all aspects of my practice. She coached me for four years. During those years, Marnie continued to remind me to stop apologising for the way in which the Universe was inspiring me to work. She told me that I would thrive when I chose to work with clients that valued my unique way of doing Reiki, and that it was okay if there were people who didn't resonate with my style of practising Reiki. She advised that I should aim to work with people who would love to receive both Reiki and intuitive guidance. Much to my surprise, I realised that there are many people who, like me, are fascinated by the world of spirit, energy and healing. Under Marnie's guidance and encouragement, I was able to move from a situation in which I was previously "allowed" to pass on intuitive messages only when practising as a medium, but not "allowed" to do so as a Reiki practitioner, to doing both comfortably and confidently at the same time.

When I began working with Marnie, I was operating under the business name, *Reiki Workshops WA*, which was founded in 2009. In 2017 I re-branded my business to become *Intuitive Reiki International,* with a global vision to mainstream Intuitive Reiki and to create a movement that would inspire, educate and empower people to awaken their intuition through learning Reiki. I was able to work from a place of love without the fear that I was doing something wrong. I finally felt complete and it was liberating!

Marnie also asked me why I was reluctant to teach my students to the Reiki Master level. Recognising my lack of self-belief, she encouraged me to get out of my own way and to start helping people to be the best version of themselves. I was encouraged to stop playing small and to expand my business to include teaching and training Reiki at the master level.

Marnie helped me to shape and create a new integrated business model which clearly conveyed to the world that my practice was more than just running Reiki energy. I was given the professional freedom and confidence to run my Reiki practice, while at the same time, to share intuitive messages with clients. Although Marnie began as my business coach, she went on to become a great friend and mentor for whom I will be forever grateful.

LIVING FROM THE HEART

The Science of the Heart

What is the heart energy field and why would you want to access it? While most of my knowledge in this field comes from experiences I have had with my clients, there is a vast amount of scientific research that has now been conducted on the physical and energetic aspects of the heart. According to HeartMath Institute ("HMI"), research has shown that the human heart has similar functions to our brain in that it has over 40,000 neurotransmitters, possessing both short and long-term memory, and which records and relays information from the heart to the brain. In fact, the heart brain sends more information and signals to the brain than the brain sends to the heart. HMI's Dr.

J. Andrew Armour discovered that the heart has a complex nervous system and supports cells just like the brain does and acts independently to the brain. Dr Armour qualified the heart as a "little brain" and termed it the "heart brain."

Research done by HMI has also shown that the signals the human heart sends to the brain can influence our perception, emotion and mental processes, and that the heart has a magnetic energy field that can be measured several feet away from the body, having a direct effect on its surroundings. Simply put, while the heart's magnetic field changes in accordance with your emotions, others can pick up on and be affected by those emotions through the magnetic field alone. In addition, while positive emotions have a positive and calming effect on the physical body, negative emotions have been proven to create chaos within the nervous system of the human body. When we experience uplifting emotions such as appreciation, joy, care, and love, our heart rhythm pattern becomes highly ordered and coherent. Coherent heart rhythms help the brain to focus, create greater connections and allow for more innovative and creative problem solving. [3]

The Heart and Intuitive Reiki

When you are attuned and practising and living by the Reiki principles, your heart becomes naturally coherent. When you are channelling Reiki energy your magnetic field is filled with positive energy, which in turn, positively

---

[3] HeartMath Institute. (2023), Expanding Our Capacity to Love. *Global Coherence Initiative.*
https://www.heartmath.org/gci/

influences your life experiences. For instance, imagine yourself waking in the morning and starting the day by giving yourself Reiki and focusing on one of the Reiki principles – *just for today, be grateful for your many blessings*. With a new focus, you begin to think about your family and something about them that you are grateful for. It could be the cup of tea that your husband makes for you, or the perfect health and well-being of your children. Such thoughts fill your heart with positive emotions. Your brain responds to these impulses and in turn, regulates your body to be in a state of wellbeing and peace. Your magnetic field is filled with positive energy throughout your day, attracting only those experiences which reflect the same energy within your magnetic field - positive opportunities and experiences that might otherwise not have been available to you. Not only do the positive emotions attract positive experiences, but your immune system is also given an energetic boost as well.

I remember an incident I had with Gerald a few years ago which demonstrates the effect living by the Reiki principles and heart coherence has on our experiences. We had arrived home from work. Both of us had a very challenging and frustrating day, so we decided to go for a walk before dinner, thinking it would make us feel better. As we walked out the door, we weren't in the best of moods, to say the least, and we began to complain about the events of the day. Before I knew it, I started to notice Gerald and I were walking totally out of sync. He was walking far too fast for me, which made me even more annoyed than I already was. At the same time, whenever I asked him to slow down, he became increasingly frustrated. As a result, we ended up walking separately and in silence for most of the way home. Living by the Reiki principles was obviously not on the forefront of our minds, and it showed. We were totally out of alignment both physically, mentally and emotionally. When we arrived home, we didn't feel any better. In fact, we felt worse than when we left.

The next day, feeling much happier after our working day, we again decided to go for a walk. This time it was different. During our walk, we reflected on all the positives of the day, and talked about how blessed we were. There was no anger. There was no worry. Our hearts were open and coherent, and it showed. Gerald and I were in perfect sync with no one walking in the front and no one lagging behind - just walking and talking in rhythm and in tune with each other. Unlike the day before, we even noticed the beauty of the trees and the singing of the birds. When we returned home, we felt inspired, uplifted and loved.

Reiki stimulates positive emotions and helps you to connect with others and deepens your connection with yourself. It requires you to slow down from the demands of life and to be present in each moment, allowing your heart to open and to feel the magnetic field of others. At the same time, those around you are able to sense and be influenced by your magnetic field of positivity. Reiki increases your ability to connect and interact in meaningful ways with others. In addition, by emitting the energy of love and acceptance, you are able to allow greater healing to take place. The effect of Reiki is palpable, as many of my students and clients report having better relationships, finding more time for others, and experiencing better overall well-being through having more patience.

The Power of Touch

As previously noted, a Reiki treatment involves placing of the hands on the recipient's body. There are twelve standard hand positions which are applied to the majority of the meridians and cover all the major organs as well as the seven main chakra systems of the body. Generally, each position is held for approximately four minutes, with a session typically lasting about forty-five minutes. As the Reiki practitioner lays their hands on another, Reiki energy flows from the practitioner's hands and a connection is made between the practitioner and the recipient. In my experience, recipients are often able to feel this energy, which leaves them feeling calm and peaceful. More significantly, this connection stimulates the body's immune system, which in time, brings about healing.

Research has shown that skin-to-skin contact is critical for maintaining mental, emotional and physical well-being. One of the most significant effects of gentle touch is reducing stress, which allows the immune system to properly function. For instance, touch has the ability to slow the pace of the nervous system, thereby calming the heart rate and blood pressure. It also has the ability to reduce feelings of loneliness and pain.[4]

Another process which demonstrates the power of touch is known as Kangaroo care. Kangaroo care was developed in the late 1970s in Bogota, Columbia, in response to the high death rate of premature babies. The process

---

[4] Sharkey L, Lamoreux K. (2021), What Does It Mean to Be Touch Starved? Healthline.
https://www.healthline.com/health/touch-starved

required the baby's parents to hold their premature baby close to their chests, skin to skin. Researchers found that this skin-to-skin contact between mother/father and baby dramatically improved the health of the baby. In particular, studies showed that the process of Kangaroo care had a positive impact on the health of the baby. For instance, such care helped to stabilize the baby's heart rate, improve the baby's breathing and sleep patterns, and oxygen levels, which resulted in earlier hospital discharges.[5]

Power vs Force

When you embark on the Intuitive Reiki journey with me, you will receive an attunement to Reiki and be taught a step-by-step process to work with the Universal Life Force Energy for your own healing and for supporting the healing of others. You will learn techniques that will attune you to the highest vibration possible for you at the time. You will learn how to give Reiki to yourself and will be encouraged to do so daily. Through daily practice, you will learn and hopefully master, gently moving out of the stream of thoughts which clutter your everyday life, to coming back into the present moment. Many of my students feel such peace when they first learn Reiki, and I believe it is because they find a bit of relief to step out of their critical and judgemental minds for a while, put a pause on the past and the future, and move into the powerful *now* and just be. Being present during Reiki is a critical component to tap

---

[5] Cleveland Clinic. (2020). Kangaroo Care. *Cleveland Clinic.* https://my.clevelandclinic.org/health/treatments/12578-kangaroo-care

into your intuition; these are the moments in which you are able to catch a glimpse of your truly unique and powerful soul. The journey to self-love and spiritual awakening then begins. Intuitive Reiki can help you to first understand and then move through your limiting beliefs. It can then assist you to find clarity and solutions to any issues or problems you may have.

Giving myself Reiki feels like I am being embraced by an energy of acceptance and unconditional love; Reiki flows through me, inspiring me to elevate my thinking to a place of appreciation. Think of it like gifting yourself with a forty-five-minute meditation that feels effortless and totally enjoyable.

One of the other benefits of learning Intuitive Reiki is the ongoing support you will receive. You will be introduced to a beautiful community of people who really want to make a difference in the world, inspiring others and helping themselves too. Intuitive Reiki brings people together in the most incredible way, creating deep and enriching soul connections and lifelong friendships.

Finally, while the Intuitive Reiki journey begins as a self-healing journey this, in and of itself, will have significant impact on others.

The late psychiatrist David R. Hawkins, M.D conducted a study using Kinesiology to explore the nature of true power. In his book, Power versus Force, Hawkins found that individuals who have undergone their own healing journey emit a powerful energy that comes from the spirit. He discovered that the nature of true power is always spiritual and that those who raise their energy and calibrate at different levels can counterbalance the weaknesses of those below them.

According to Hawkins' findings, individuals who calibrate at various levels can counterbalance the weaknesses of those below them as follows:

- Enlightenment (calibration level of 700-1000) counterbalances individuals below level 200
- Peace (calibration level of 600) counterbalances 10 million individuals
- Joy (calibration level of 540)
- Love (calibration level of 500) counterbalances 750,000 individuals
- Reason (calibration level of 400) counterbalances 400,000 individuals
- Acceptance (calibration level of 350)
- Willingness (calibration level of 310) counterbalances 90,000 individuals
- Neutrality (calibration level of 250)

Negative human emotions and their corresponding vibration levels are found below Neutrality. Hawkins' study suggests that even a few people vibrating at high levels during the day can counterbalance negative thoughts. This popular notion suggests that by raising our own vibration, we can not only experience personal benefits, but we can also contribute to raising the vibration of the entire planet. Because of our interconnectedness, we can achieve this by increasing our understanding and capacity for love and compassion.[6]

Working with Reiki can help you to increase your vibration to levels which can have a positive impact on your life as well as others.

---

[6] Gur, T. (2023) Power vs. Fore: Summary Review & Takeaways. *Elevate society.* https://elevatesociety.com/takeaways-power-vs-force/

BEYOND THE BASICS

Grounding Your Energy

Grounding is a process that brings you back into balance not only on the physical level, but on emotional and spiritual levels. It is a critical step before channelling Intuitive Reiki or doing any type of healing work as it helps the practitioner to connect with their own intuition as well as the energy of the recipient. It is a strategy which helps you to get anchored in the present moment. Having said that, one of the most common issues I find with my beautiful healers and light workers is that they spend more time in other spaces and times, and forget to focus on the current situation at hand. Therefore, before beginning any Reiki class or practice, I always take them through an exercise to assist them to ground themselves.

One exercise which I find very effective is to take a walk

outside and connect with nature. I usually take my shoes off and feel the grass beneath my feet. I look around, feel the sun on my back, listen to the sounds all around me, and then see how far and wide I can send my awareness out, observing and taking in as much of the environment as I can. There are so many techniques for grounding yourself and I suggest you work with a variety to keep the practice interesting.

White Lighting

Another important step before channelling Reiki is to visualise and mentally call in the light. While there are various ways in which to do so, many practitioners visualise a sphere of white light surrounding their body as a means to protect them from so called negative energy. I believe this method of protection only highlights any fear they are feeling; the focus is on the negative or fear-based thoughts, rather than on accessing the love and light that is within us all.

Alternatively, I teach my students to white light themselves. It's a simple process which takes place after grounding and which first requires you to slow the constant chatter of your mind and to focus on the present. I then place my hands on my body, take three deep breaths and tune into my body until I can feel the energy of Reiki flowing from my hands. Once I connect to Reiki and my body, I start to feel my energy field expand. Being a highly visual person, I then imagine pure white light radiating and expanding within me. When this occurs, waves of positive energy begin to flow through me and I am able to feel a range of emotions such as peace, excitement, joy, appreciation, and love. At this point, my body is overflowing with and is surrounded by positive energy. I know then, I am in a safe place and ready to connect with my client; I imagine wrapping light around their body and then back around mine, giving my client an energetic hug, so to speak. Once this is done, the Reiki session is ready to begin.

When you raise your vibration using the imagery of white light, you are better able to open your heart and expand your awareness. As a result, you are able to energetically and intuitively connect with another. With practice and in time, you will gain the ability to expand your light/vibration far and wide, positively influencing your surroundings and experiences.

More than Running Energy

When you are running Reiki energy, you will find yourself naturally entering into a beautiful, nurturing meditative state. In this relaxed trance-like state, intuitive insights can begin to come through. During the first few years of practising Reiki, I enjoyed the feeling of running energy and really didn't want to hear from the spirit world. I knew receiving messages from the spirit world was a possibility, because my Reiki Master, Jacqueline, had developed this skill and would pass on messages during her Reiki sessions. However, in the beginning, I was just happy to be in the moment, running energy and focusing on the client.

Later I discovered that Intuitive Reiki opens the aura of both the recipient and practitioner; both receive the light and energy, which allows a connection to Source to take place and provides a higher perspective of the situation/

person at hand. I developed the ability to easily drop into my heart and my solar plexus, which allows me to connect through my soul to access higher levels of consciousness and receive messages or intuitive insights. From that higher perspective, I view everyone I work with as an incredible human being who is worthy of my love, compassion and attentiveness.

In addition, I realised that Reiki is a gift that allows you to help yourself and someone else feel relief from the stresses of life both at the same time. One of the most beautiful aspects about Reiki is that, as we give to another, we also receive.

In the Presence of Love

"In the presence of love" is such a simple phrase and yet, the experience of feeling profound love, can change your life completely. Intuitive Reiki has allowed me to experience and to live from this place of unconditional love. For instance, during my workshops teaching Reiki, in particular, during the third or fourth attunements, I am quite often overcome with huge emotions of love for my students. Just like the sun shines for us all, so too does unconditional love - Reiki's Universal Life Force Energy. While some people feel it and say "yes" in that moment, others may experience such love at a later date, when they are ready and choose to accept it.

I distinctly remember the first time I saw one of my students through the presence of the Christ energy. I felt Jesus with me. His presence was always in energy form and I remember feeling this magnificent light gently blend with mine. When I opened my eyes, I was holding my student's hands. During the process of this most sacred experience, I saw my beautiful student through the eyes of the Christ light. I had tears of joy streaming down my face because I wanted my student to know that she was absolutely perfect just the way she was.

In those precious moments following the attunements, I sit with my class and listen to each person's account of what they experienced. The most beautiful heart opening and healing conversations take place. My students often feel the presence of love and acceptance for who they are; they reflect upon the journey their life has taken to get them to the point where they are, sitting in a room with me and their new Reiki friends. Many are able to release any suffering they have endured as they experience the energy and vibration of unconditional love blessing them. The experience is so powerful because they are brought to an awareness of their own soul's light and love.

I recall a new student, Anna, who approached me with a huge smile on her face after receiving an attunement. She explained that during the attunement she had tears of joy streaming down her face as she was overcome with a sense of love and worthiness; filled with that loving presence, Anna shared that she found herself extending that same love and compassion to her fellow students. She said, "…it was a feeling of coming home to myself;" and an experience which she would always remember.

As each student relays their experience, a softness flows through me, at which time I give guidance and help them to understand what they experienced. Often, I am then able to channel my guides to help them understand their experience of the attunement, and to guide them on their healing journey.

Working with Christ Light

As you now know, while attuning my students to Reiki, I often feel I'm not working alone. I wasn't always aware of the energy that worked with me when I first started teaching Reiki. I just had a truly positive feeling and trusted that it felt right for me. I couldn't clairvoyantly see the beings of light that assisted me, but I could feel their energy and blessing. My left hand would be open to receiving the Reiki energy, and my right hand would be giving the attunement to my students.

One day while I was teaching a lovely lady who was doing her Reiki Master training with me, I called on my mentor Rayeleen, who was also a Reiki Master and a gifted clairvoyant as well, to assist me in demonstrating the attunement process to my student. Both Rayeleen and I took a moment to tune into our bodies and the Reiki energy. As I started the attunement process, my left hand went out to receive the Reiki energy and my right hand proceeded with the attunement process. After I had finished the first demonstration, Rayeleen gently asked, "Do you know who's holding your hand, Lisa?"

I responded, "No, I just feel energy."

Rayeleen then proceeded to tell me that Jesus was holding my hand. I didn't think much of it at the time as I was more concerned about teaching my student. After the attunements were done and the session with my student was over, Rayeleen stated that she kept receiving the name of Jesus throughout the day and explained that with Jesus by my side during attunements, I am able to assist my students to make big shifts in their lives for their higher good.

I spent some time in disbelief of what Rayeleen had conveyed, but at the same time, it made so much sense, and I deeply admired and trusted Rayeleen. When I finally came to terms with it all, I was ready to receive the love of Jesus and to begin working more consciously with his energy. I felt so very blessed, however, it was not something I was ready to tell my students. I could only imagine what others would think if I told them that I am a Reiki Master who channels Jesus. I was afraid that I would be ridiculed or that I would be viewed as egotistical. At that stage in my life, I wanted to be as humble as I could be and to disclose this aspect of me just didn't feel right.

Furthermore, I wasn't brought up to be religious, and so was not aware of the details of Jesus's life. However, I knew enough about him; an ascended master spirit guide who is a high-vibrational, enlightened being of love and light, willing to work with anyone who feels inspired to call on his frequency and vibration. I didn't want others to think that Reiki or I was associated with a particular religion or faith. Reiki is non-denominational and is open to all faiths. We simply work with light in whatever form it appears to us. Hence, I decided that as long as my students felt the love and blessing of the energy, there was no need for them to know who was standing by my side.

When I told Gerald I was working with Jesus, he just said, "That's cool," which was his usual response to things that would totally blow my mind. It turns out that it was my own judgement that created my discomfort, and no one else's. When I finally felt called to tell groups of students, they were supportive and excited. There was no judgement or ridicule.

The more I taught Reiki, the more I was inspired to teach from a place of pure alignment. As my intuition became clearer, so did my connection to Jesus. To this day, I can feel him come through when I work with Reiki and during all my attunements. Jesus blesses each of my students and harmonises us as a group. Quite often I am moved to tears. His energy that flows through and with me is of pure love and grace, and so very humble and kind.

Attuned with the Christ Consciousness

In January 2023, I had the most inspiring experience teaching my Reiki 2 students. I had finished teaching the Reiki symbols to the class, and was preparing the students for the attunement process. Before the attunement, I asked the students to set an intention regarding what they would like to achieve during the attunement. After every student had been attuned, I asked them to go outside and gather in small groups to share their attunement experience. One by one, each student shared their experience, and although each experience was special, there was one that I'll never forget.

Jody, who was a quiet student in the class, shared that before the attunement had commenced, she initially asked to have an intuitive experience and to see spirit. However, she re-considered and decided that she would, instead, surrender to the moment and be present and open to the experience. Although her eyes were closed during the attunement, Jody said she had a knowing that it was me attuning her. She said she felt very peaceful. She went on to explain that as I moved in front of her body and held her hand, something weird occurred. I told her that the weirder the better, and smiled a warm smile so that she knew she was safe to share her story with the group. Jody continued and said that while I was attuning her to Reiki, she saw in her mind's eye, Jesus superimposed right where I was standing. She explained that she wasn't at all religious, and therefore, the image of Jesus took her by surprise. She said, "What followed was an intense feeling of unconditional love and I had tears streaming down my face. I was quite surprised that I started crying, but it wasn't because something was wrong. It was because I felt so loved…I wasn't feeling particularly emotional, just peaceful and happy to be learning Reiki."

I later shared with Jody that I channel Jesus when I do my Reiki attunements, a practice that I don't often share with my students, as I don't want to give anyone the impression that Reiki is influenced by any religion or denomination. In addition to my spirit guides and angels, I call on the Christ consciousness, and feel his presence with me during all my attunements. Jody was so pleased to know that I worked with Jesus, for it validated her experience as true. In addition, I was given the gift of knowing that I am and have always been supported and loved by many benevolent beings of light.

Love vs Fear

Intuitive Reiki is an awakening to, or a remembering of all that we are. Through the programming and conditioning of life, we have energetically separated ourselves from our inner knowing, and many people I meet are living primarily from the head. Intuitive Reiki brings our awareness back into our hearts and turns up the energy for us to feel it.

When you are in alignment with Reiki, you are in a state of bliss. There is no fear, because fear in its many forms is simply an absence of light. When your mind focuses on fear, it can feel very real indeed. However, we always have a choice. You can focus on the fear until it becomes bigger than life. Or you can choose to focus on the energy of grace, love and kindness as an energetic presence that is within you every single moment of every single day; a presence many have forgotten. Intuitive Reiki is the practice that can help you to remember.

Your connection to source and unconditional love will become stronger, the more often you engage in the practice of Intuitive Reiki. You'll discover that a spiritual solution exists to any problem you may have, and it comes from love. When you choose to love, your focus shifts, and answers to your problems are revealed to you when you are open and receptive. Many times, they will come to you as a matter of course, with ease and grace. I'll give you an example.

I had a student, Jenny, who told me that she decided to learn Reiki after reading a book called *You Can Heal Your Life* by Louise Hay. Jenny shared with me that she had recently received treatment for a cancerous tumour, and that while the doctors were able to treat the tumour, they also advised her that there was no known cure for the form of cancer that she had, and that it was quite possible the cancer would return. Although she meditated regularly, fear set in. Through reading Hay's book, Jenny realised that the cure for illness can be found within; that we have the power within to heal our body through our connection to our mind, body and spirit. As a result, Jenny ventured to deepen her connection with her spirit guides and to learn more about self-healing and Reiki.

Jenny had several Reiki sessions with me and shared that, unless it was necessary, she chose not to tell anyone that she had cancer. Even though Jenny was symptom free, she was living in a state of fear that her cancer would return. In order to manage her supressed fears, she started to drink alcohol and to engage in other unhealthy lifestyle choices to cope with that fear. Jenny was so worried about the future prospect of the cancer returning, so much so, she was unable to enjoy her current situation of being in good health. She was unable to live in the present.

Over time and with the help of Reiki and spiritual guidance, Jenny gradually accepted her past and was grateful for all that had transpired to lead her to where she was in her life. She began to love every layer of her being – mental, physical and spiritual. I witnessed a real shift in Jenny's attitude and outlook on life – from fear to optimism and love. She was able to finally accept and embrace the fact that she was in remission. Through Reiki, Jenny released the fear and was no longer hostage to her health situation. She had taken her power back.

Knowing I have a choice to choose love over fear has provided me with a sense of freedom and authenticity. When I choose love over fear, I remember my divine nature, and to surrender to the will of God - to surrender to my higher calling and to listen to the inner whisperings of my own pure and loving heart. I trust that I am always guided by this unseen power.

Through my own journey, I know that you can truly awaken to such love and divine potential to live a full and happy life. Reiki opens the door to intuition and creates an essence and a presence of pure love that you can tune into any second of any day and be gifted with a totally new and vastly beautiful capacity to see life through the eyes of Source. Through walking the path of Intuitive Reiki, your anger will soften, your fears will lessen, and your compassion will deepen. You will find a gentler, kinder self with whom you will have many a conversation within your mind and your heart. You will start making decisions in life that serve your own individual joy and begin saying no to the things that no longer fulfil you. Any pain you have endured will begin to subside. You will make new friendships based on trust, love and compassion for each life. You will have an energy that will flow through your body, which will heal and change the very structure of the physical body, if that is your path which serves your highest good. Intuitive Reiki will guide you to tune into your greatest potential to start living a purposeful life.

Soul Awareness

The soul is the inner essence of a person. It is unique to each and every individual and is often referred to as the higher self. In addition, although the "soul" is also often used interchangeably with "spirit," the spirit is that part of an individual or sentient being which is eternal and one with the Universe. It is the soul which connects you to spirit. For instance, the saying "she is an old soul" refers to a person who has had many incarnations and with each incarnation, carries certain aspects of previous lives, which in turn, influences who they are in the current life. A person with an old soul often possesses innate wisdom, which they have not acquired through the current life, but rather, through lessons learned in past lives. The soul, your higher self, is the guiding light that links us to the Universal Life Force Energy. It is the inner voice that is always calling you home to yourself, where we discover who we truly are. The stronger your connection to your soul, the stronger your connection to spirit.

Through the practice of Intuitive Reiki, you become more aware of your soul or higher self. In essence, Intuitive Reiki encourages you to listen to the internal whisperings of your soul. The practice of Intuitive Reiki provides you with the ability to sense and see your life and the lives of others from the soul's perspective – a perspective that is free from the confines of the mind or ego, and instead, is filled with love and compassion.

I believe that when you are connected to your higher self, you are better able to heal yourself as well as to assist others to heal, for it is from this basis you are then able to connect to the spiritual realm – Source, God, the all that is. Intuitive Reiki is a practice that provides the practitioner with the opportunity to connect to the soul of the recipient and to offer spiritual guidance to them while running healing energy at the same time. It is a process in which messages from spirit are conveyed to the recipient to help heal any issues the recipient is experiencing.

Reiki is also an invitation to practice living from the heart and to recognise the callings of your soul. When we can understand ourselves from this higher perspective, then we open ourselves up to receive the guidance and wisdom from the spiritual realm, God or higher consciousness.

Source Energy vs Psychic Energy

When working with Reiki you are working with and through your soul to attune or connect yourself to Universal Life Force Energy – Source energy. When you call in this energy, it first fills your whole being with light and powerful healing energy. For many practitioners, the energy is experienced mostly as heat coming from their hands. The energy is then transferred to the recipient when the practitioner's hands are placed on the recipient's body.

Source energy surrounds us all and is unlimited. It is omnipresent. Although it does not require any effort to access, it does require an openness to receive, without judgement and expectation. I like to think of it like the sun, always shining, and it is up to us to choose to step out of the shade and into the sun to bask in the energy it provides.

In contrast, when you are working with psychic energy, you are consciously choosing to send your own personal energy to another. It is the energy we use when we are relating to others on a human level. It can be used to tune into the field of light that can be seen or sensed by another, commonly called the aura or the field that surrounds the body. Our aura contains within it all our personal experiences. Our ego or personality also has energy that we can access. Therefore, when we relate to another, there is always an exchange of psychic energy. The level of exchange is of varying degrees and intensity and depends on the receptivity and empathic nature of each person.

Psychic energy can be given and taken many times without our knowing. Years ago, I read *The Celestine Prophecy* by James Redfield, which describes the way we interact with people on a psychic level. It explains how the ego will use control dramas to manipulate others to gain energy. In this regard, you will always know when you have been with someone who elevates you or depletes your energy by the way you feel after spending time with them.

In contrast, Intuitive Reiki will align you with Source energy. When you tune in and use Source energy, you are able to bring through high-level guidance; you feel elevated and are left with more energy than when you first began. Through Intuitive Reiki, you will learn that no one can deplete you when you are connected to the infinite Reiki energy. In addition, you will learn to take responsibility for your thoughts and your feelings. You will learn how to embrace empowering thoughts and drop the negative stories the mind creates. Learning how to manage your mind is made so much easier when you have access to unlimited Source energy, and can go within at any time to tune in and receive the light and love this energy has to offer.

To illustrate, I recall practising a new energy healing technique that I had recently learned. I asked Marnie if she would allow me to practise this new technique on her, and she agreed. We met one evening, and I began by giving her Reiki, gently guiding her into the quantum realm. Her state of consciousness expanded very quickly, and while we were open to whatever transpired during the process, neither of us was ready for what we experienced that night.

Marnie described seeing an opening that looked like a portal of some kind. When I asked her what it felt like, she said it felt good. As a result, she decided to go through the portal to see where it led her. As she stepped through, her consciousness expanded and she entered a deep trance state and started channelling messages from a new spirit guide that she met through the meditation. This was totally unexpected. We later discovered Marnie's new spirit guide was named Christian. During the channelling session, Christian relayed the message that Marnie would need some support with learning to channel and that I would need to be open to more wisdom and guidance. After the session ended, we were both quite surprised at what had taken place, and eager to further explore this new-found technique.

After the first few sessions, Marnie told me that she felt exhausted after her initial experience. We realised that Marnie was using a lot of her psychic energy to connect and bring Christian through. Christian explained to us that it was important to use Reiki to build the energy as well as to call in the light so that we could open a pure channel between Marnie and me. Acting upon Christian's suggestion, we realised that once we connected to each other through Reiki, we were able raise our vibration and connect to our respective souls and access higher states of consciousness, building a strong connection with her guide and mine. During our sessions, we were given answers to our daily problems and provided with insights into life from a spiritual perspective. In addition, instead of feeling exhausted, each session left us feeling empowered and energised.

Healing Connections

What I love most about Reiki, especially Intuitive Reiki, is that we are given a spiritual gift which allows us to hold a divine healing space for another, while at the same time healing ourselves. If you've been in one of my classes, then you know that I have an unwavering belief that each of us as sovereign beings can only heal ourselves; that we do not have the capacity to heal another. Rather, through the channelling of Reiki, the recipients are supported on every level of their being to heal themselves. Reiki guides them to turn the light on in the dark recesses of their mind, heart and soul until they are ready to express or release their pain/limiting beliefs, whether emotional, physical or spiritual.

More significantly, practising Intuitive Reiki allows us to experience deep and profound connections with others. Recipients have a tendency to feel loved and safe while receiving Reiki; they allow themselves to be vulnerable, which is necessary to heal. Witnessing others healing themselves is one of the most incredible and inspiring positions to be in. Your heart will crack open to experience waves of love for them as you soften and gently guide them out of pain and into love, together sharing in something truly beautiful.

It's important to add that if someone shares a traumatic event with you, you gently let them know that it can be really helpful for them to seek additional support from a trained specialist who can also help them with any unresolved feelings associated with the trauma or event that surfaced during your session. Often a client will continue to see you for Reiki, as well as see another practitioner to help them with the trauma. It is not uncommon for a person to work with a team of health care providers, including the family doctor, psychologist or counsellor, and a Reiki practitioner.

I believe that this kind of emotional sharing happens when you have created a trust and bond with your clients, which usually forms after getting to know them through providing them with regular Reiki sessions. I have had many clients who have been able to release some long held pain and deep shame and resentment that has led to them feeling liberated and free from the trauma of their past, allowing for them to lead happier and fulfilled lives.

PERSONAL GROWTH FROM REIKI

Surrender

I recall the very first time I was introduced to the term "surrender". I was in a session with my Reiki Master, Jacqueline, who explained to me what it means to surrender. I was taught that working with Reiki can help us to let go of the need to control the outcome of situations or circumstances presented in our lives, and instead, begin to trust life. This process is especially significant when we are faced with challenges, which are out of our control or that leave us feeling helpless despite our best efforts to create a desired outcome. It is accepting life on life's terms and trusting the process to lead you to where you are meant to be without any preconceived notions or expectations of a particular outcome.

Although this process is not necessarily an intellectual one, I believe it needs to be understood before you can truly embody all that it means to live life in surrender – to live without fear. I liken surrender to having faith - to trusting in a higher power that is here to guide us through life, rather than to dictate and tell us how to live. Surrender is a process of recognising and releasing the control of the mind or ego and giving in to the greater will of your soul. When we have mastered being in a state of surrender, then I believe we find true freedom. We are liberated from our fear-based thoughts and, as a result, are open and receptive to living life in a state of flow. Although at times it is difficult, I strive to live in a state of surrender for I have come to realise that often, what I see is not necessarily what I get; that when I'm faced with a challenging situation, what ultimately transpires is better than what I expected or is an experience that has helped me learn and grow.

After a year into writing this book, doubts about my ability to write, let alone to complete this book began to creep into my psyche. I spiralled into a state of fear and ruminated on thoughts of, "*It's too hard. I'm not good enough to write this book. It's a mammoth project which will take too long to complete.*" I gradually lost my inspiration to write and, instead, found myself focusing on other things. No matter how hard I tried to get myself back to writing this book, I just couldn't.

Then one day, I tuned in and asked myself why I was feeling so much resistance, to which I received the message, "There is no answer to that question, Lisa." I pondered the answer, and then thought perhaps I needed to ask another question, "Why don't I want to write this book right now?" Again, there was no answer.

Hitting a metaphorical brick wall, I released self-judgement and accepted the fact that I didn't feel like writing. I surrendered to what was, accepting that perhaps it was perfect that I took this break from writing; that my resistance was not wrong. It was just resistance. When I gave myself some space, I gradually and very gently came to the realisation that I needed to re-set my thinking and remember the reasons I wanted to write this book in the first place. I knew when I first started, I had been inspired to share my journey with Reiki and intuition, which in turn, has taught me to live with so much more peace, joy, and love in my life. Once I surrendered and took the pressure off myself, I felt so much more at peace and trusted that when the time was right to write again, I would.

Psychic Protection, Self-Love and Light

While there is always an exchange of energy in our interactions with others, it is our responsibility to look after our own energy and how we expend our energy. This is called psychic protection. I believe that psychic protection is more about self-love and holding yourself in a place of true reverence.

One of the best ways to protect yourself is to fill your own cup first, and to be very aware of how you respond to people or situations that impact you. I have found that when I take the time to honour myself and to do what makes me happy, I naturally become happier, more likable and enjoyable to be around. Life seems to flow with greater ease and grace. Reiki has taught me to honour myself and understand that when we do what we enjoy, our vibration naturally rises. Practising Reiki is a natural high for me, and I know in my heart that, over the years, my level of consciousness and vibration has increased and will continue to do so. Elevating our consciousness and raising our vibration is the best form of psychic protection that we can have.

Another way to protect your psychic energy is through connecting to the light or to align with love. By actively choosing throughout the day to align with love or to call in the light, you can access high level energies, which you can then utilise how and when you feel inspired. Calling in the light raises your vibration, which can prevent others from taking energy away from you and upsetting you. However, a necessary part of calling in the light to align you with Source is to be aware of your thoughts while doing so.

In the early years of my Reiki practice, every night after tucking my daughters into bed, I would imagine them surrounded by a ball of beautiful white light. Although I had every good intention of visualising the white light around them, the basis of that intention stemmed from a deep-seated fear of the spirit world. At the time, I started to see and sense spirit clairvoyantly, and although I was aware that Reiki protected me from negative thought forms, I was still afraid of the spirit world.

After surrounding my daughters with white light for a few weeks, I realised what was happening. My fears were manifesting – the greater the fear, the more often I would see and sense spirit, which would then create more fear. I was focusing on what I was protecting them from, rather than the light itself. My thoughts in those moments of surrounding them in white light were not aligned with love, but were, in fact, producing more and more fear. I immediately changed my tactic and focused only on the light, without fear.

One day in my early Reiki years, while I was working with Rayeleen at *Yes2Life*, I had decided to head over to the shopping centre to buy myself a coffee. Before I left, I mentioned to Rayeleen that I was going to "white light" myself before I crossed the road. Rayeleen looked at me with genuine curiosity and asked me why I felt the need to do so. I replied, "To protect myself from all the negative and angry people that might be over there." As a sensitive soul, at the time I felt I was able to pick up and tune into people's pain. Although this was true, I was unaware of how I was using my sensitivity.

I had been involved in an incident in which I had been berated by one of the shop owners at the shopping centre. While working at Starlight, hospital volunteers and I would erect temporary stalls at various shopping centres on what was called national "Star Day" to sell merchandise and raise funds in support of Starlight, and to bring awareness to the public about Starlight's cause. On one particular Star Day, we were assigned to open up a stall at the shopping centre across the road from *Yes2Life*. I was also asked to represent Starlight as Captain Starlight. The stall was stationed directly across a donut shop, and although other volunteers were manning the stall throughout the day, my stint was only for a couple of hours. I began to greet and chat to patrons passing by to greet and chat to patrons passing by. Then after about an hour, the owner of the donut shop marched over to me and began to complain about what I was doing; with a raised voice, he stated that I was distracting business away from his shop and that we should relocate our stall. Much to his dismay, I advised him that we couldn't move as the shopping centre management had placed us there, and therefore, the situation was clearly out of our control. He wasn't very happy, and as a result, he continued to rant in my face for what seemed several minutes. I was quite shaken by his aggressiveness and unfortunately, never forgot that experience. I feared either seeing him again, or having another unpleasant experience at the shopping centre. Therefore, I believed that if I surrounded myself with light, I would be less fearful and shielded from any negative occurrences.

Rayeleen smiled at me when I shared my explanation and then proceeded to tell me her take on working with the light whenever she went to the shopping centre. She explained that she always begins her stroll to the shopping centre by first appreciating the beautiful sunshine. As she walks across the carpark adjacent to the shopping centre, she then opens her heart up to Reiki, which she can access every minute of every day. She visualises herself as a channel of pure divine love, and as she walks through the shopping centre, she looks for places to project that love. Because her thoughts are aligned to love and gratitude, Rayeleen explained to me that the most amazing things would happen on her little shopping trips. She would bump into beautiful customers that she hadn't seen for a while. She would notice a beautiful baby giggling with her mother in the trolley, or she would see people laughing and sharing stories over lunch or coffee.

Rayeleen's perspective on the use of white light created

a massive shift for me. I realised that harnessing empowering and loving thoughts while working with the light is the key to being in alignment with all that is positive; it is the shift from fear to love. Coffee trips from that day forward became one of my greatest joys, and I never encountered a negative experience at that shopping centre again.

Listen to Your Body

Many of my clients seek Reiki to assist them in healing physical and emotional issues. Our bodies are excellent indicators of any underlying beliefs or causes of those issues and, during a Reiki session, I am intuitively guided to how my client can release the emotion connected to the issue at hand.

I have had several experiences in which I have avoided addressing an emotional issue only to later have something happen to me which forces me to address the issue. Remember the several occasions I struggled to write this book? During one period, running my business had become so demanding, consuming all my attention. I felt like there wasn't enough time in the day to do all the things my business required, let alone spend quality time with my family. I felt like a hamster on a wheel. Consequently, I began to lose the joy in the work that I was doing, and writing this book was beginning to feel like another chore, one that I didn't feel I had the time or the motivation to do. I harboured negative thoughts regarding my ability to complete this book, and together with the demands of my business, I was left agitated and exhausted.

Then one day while I was at home with my family,

my daughter unexpectedly offered friends of hers and their family to stay with us to escape a fire burning out of control near their home. Although I was happy to provide a safe place for this family to stay, our dog, Rosie, was not impressed as they also brought their not-so-friendly dog with them. After a nonstop round of barking and growling, the visiting dog proceeded to charge towards Rosie and backed her up against the wall. I scooped Rosie up out of harm's way, and in doing so, I smashed my finger into the wall. It was so painful and I was in agony throughout the night. The next day, I went to the doctor who confirmed that my ring finger on my right hand was broken. As a result, I was referred to the hospital for treatment.

When I arrived at the hospital, the waiting area was filled, and I waited for three hours before being seen. During that time, I started to relax a bit, and slowly realised that my belief of not having enough time to do everything was just an illusion. While sitting in the waiting room, surprisingly, I found the time. Not being able to type, I began to respond to the long list of emails in my inbox with phone calls. The time in the waiting room allowed me to slow down and reflect on the reasons I do what I do. More importantly, I realised that I broke my finger because I was operating in a chaotic state and was out of energetic alignment. Curious, I later wondered what my broken ring finger symbolised spiritually, and whether it meant I had an energetic or emotional block that I was avoiding, but needed to address. Here is what I found:

The Hidden Meaning Behind Your Ring Finger

"The ring finger on your left hand is associated with inspiration. It represents your state of inspiration and the inner spark that awakens your fires.

The ring finger on your right hand is associated with creativity. It represents your creative potential and the ability to use your fires by connecting different ideas together and bringing them to life. But you need both of these energies to be a creator and invent something unique.

If you do not have an inspiration, you will not be able to truly create novelty no matter how much creative potential you have. If you do create, it will be forced and emotionless, almost robotic.

If you do not let your creative energy flow freely, you will not be able to direct your inspiration and create novelty, or invent something the world can evolve with, no matter how much inspiration you have.

You need to be inspired creatively so you can truly invent and create something unique and special." [7]

Breaking my finger gave me some much-needed time for inner self reflection. Unable to effectively work with my broken finger, I was forced to cancel many of my appointments. Consequently, I had much more time to myself to reflect on my life, to notice how busy I had become, and to question whether I still loved what I was doing and how I was working. I realised that I had become so busy with

---

[7] Davcevski, D. (2017). Here is What Each Finger on Your Hands Tells About Your Energy. Life coach code.
https://www.lifecoachcode.com/2017/12/04/what-each-finger-on-your-hands-tells-about-your-energy/

work that I wasn't making time for my own creativity and was starting to move away from the aspects of my work that truly brought me joy.

It was at this point I decided to reassess the work I was doing and change the manner in I which I worked. I decided to let go and delegate the overwhelming administrative duties that were bogging me down, both in time and emotionally. I had a cast fitted around my finger, and in five weeks my finger was healed. Funnily, it took a broken finger for me to create more balance in my life; I have learned that I don't need to do everything on my own, and that all which needs to be done, will be done in divine timing.

Where Attention Goes, Energy Flows

During my early years of practising Reiki, I was gifted with a powerful lesson about focus and intention. I have always had very intense emotions, and I wanted to understand and manage the many emotional ups and downs I was experiencing at the time. I wanted to open up more to, and be led by, the strength and wisdom of my heart; to learn how to honour and trust my guidance, and have the courage to act in alignment with my heart, and not so much with my ego for the sake of pleasing others.

I was extremely sensitive to others and situations, and my emotions in response were intense. Because these intense emotions often left me feeling spent and exhausted, the only way to protect myself was to disconnect and shut down. I didn't understand much of the world; there was so much hurt and suffering which affected me, and I just didn't want to feel any of it. At the time, my sensitivity felt like a curse rather than a gift. This is the life of an empath. Having this sensitivity makes for a wonderful healer, with an ability to easily connect with others, and to understand them both intuitively and emotionally. However, when an empath is unable to control the wave of emotions which they encounter, it can leave them feeling exhausted and depleted.

When I was in high school, I watched two girls in a physical fight. Although it was the most horrible thing to witness, what was worse was the circle of people gathered around, cheering the girls on and taking pleasure from seeing two girls hurting each other. Not one to take pleasure in seeing someone in pain, I just couldn't understand how and why this was happening. After witnessing that event, a feeling of sadness overcame me. I closed part of my heart to the aggressive and hostile world I often found around me in high school. As a sensitive soul, it was my way of self-preservation.

Practising Reiki has taught me that I always have two choices. One is to focus on the people and situations, which cause me pain, worry and despair. The other is to see an opportunity to hold space by sending love and Reiki, or to focus my attention on more positive situations and people. So, by watching the girls fight, I was unknowingly supporting the situation, which only made me feel worse. Had I known then what I know now, I could have walked away from the fight and focused on something more pleasant, which in turn, would have helped me avoid the unnecessary distress.

In short, "Where attention goes - energy flows." I've been reminded of this over the years through different experiences in which I felt great emotion, and at the same time, felt an inability to change or to help change a situation I was witnessing. I believe that if we are to create powerful and positive change in the world, then we need to be the ones to choose and foster more love, joy and compassion. Reiki is the perfect tool to foster these choices.

Thoughts Create Your Reality

One of the first lessons I learned through Reiki is to be mindful of your thoughts and to take responsibility for them. This is especially true when your thoughts are causing you pain and worry. It is during those times when you must question whether the thoughts which are causing you distress/stress are true or real, let alone serving the highest good for you and all concerned. I've had many experiences in which I allowed my thoughts to get the better of me, to my detriment.

During a business course I attended, I was partnered with a woman to do an exercise. Initially, I was excited to be paired with her, but when we were physically next to each other, I felt differently. The energy she gave off was very different to the vibe I was feeling. At one point, she told me I reminded her of her school principal, and the energy she exuded indicated to me that she didn't really like her principal. Hence, I immediately assumed that she didn't like me, which in turn, led me to decide that I didn't like her as well. What followed was a very uncomfortable exchange, and I looked forward to working with a different partner. When we did move to different partners, I told myself it didn't matter if she liked me or not, but it did.

I later realised that my feeling of not being liked really

had nothing to do with her. I made an assumption, whether it was true or not. I judged her, which ended up causing me a bit of angst. Her statement about her principal only brought to light the insecurity I held at the time, which I now realise was my issue and not hers. Had I recognised my thoughts and stopped them from having a life of their own, I probably would have had a much better experience at the workshop.

On a more positive note, I recall being interviewed for a global spiritual summit. After the summit I stated to my assistant that I really enjoyed being interviewed and how I would love to be interviewed more. The next day I happened to see a post by a fellow speaker from the summit who was learning how to channel, and wondered whether anyone else had learned channeling. I replied to her post and stated that, in addition to channeling, I also taught others to channel. She later contacted me, asking if she could interview me about this topic. Of course I said "yes", and two days later I was doing my second interview speaking about my love for channeling and the personal gifts that come with this practice.

As you can see, our thoughts create our perception or reality of the world. But whatever impact our thoughts may have on how we experience life, I have learned that the potential of manifesting those thoughts into reality is increased by the feelings which accompany those thoughts. Based on my experience, I now know that it is the emotional essence which comes with a thought which brings the thought to life. I was once told that the feeling is the prayer - the secret of manifesting one's dreams and desires.

Powerful Positive Intention

While thoughts can create your reality, intention is the starting point of every dream. When you harness the creative power and potential of your desires and visions, you can begin to create powerful and positive changes in your life. As a start, setting daily intentions is how you can get to be in the driver's seat of your life, rather than life working on default. Once you have set your intentions, then the next step is for you to act in fulfilling those intentions. You can then begin to manifest what it is you want in life to fulfil all your needs and desires, whatever they may be.

However, aside from setting an intention and taking action, there is one element, which I believe is paramount to manifesting what you desire. It is to let go of the need to control how that intention manifests. I'll give you an example.

One morning, while working at *Yes 2 Life,* I was going about my usual morning routine. I opened the shop, put on my favourite music, chose an essential oil for the day and lit a candle. Then I stood at the desk and took a few moments of silence to start my day with a positive intention - to learn something new.

It was a relatively normal day in the centre with lots of phone calls, beautiful customers and a few sales made. While going about my business, a gentlemen walked in. He was an older man, and what I first noticed was his beautiful blue eyes. I said "hello" and as he looked at me, a calm and peaceful feeling overcame me. He walked towards me and it was as if time stood still. In a very unusual way, everything did. The phone stopped ringing, no one came in, and the shop was clear of other staff as all wellness practitioners were in their rooms with clients. In a moment of utter silence, I felt I had entered a kind of spiritual vortex. I saw such love and compassion in his eyes, and when he looked at me, it was like he was reaching right into my soul. Normally, I would have felt very uncomfortable to have a stranger elicit such a feeling within me, but I felt completely safe and accepted in this gentleman's presence.

We spoke for about fifteen minutes and had the most beautiful conversation. He told me that he was a messenger for God, and that he followed an impulse to come into the store and speak to me. He told me that my heart would lead the way to assist many people. He saw something very special in me, and came in specifically to tell me that he believed in me with what I would do later in life. He didn't buy anything, and after relaying his message from God, he left.

I never did see that man again. I felt like I had a personal encounter with an earth angel and was given a spiritual blessing on that day. I certainly learned something new, but not in the way I imagined. By setting a clear intention that morning, I was gifted with an unexpected encounter with a stranger who gave me an unforgettable message – that I was unique and was going to make a difference in the world. Because of him, I learned that I could create anything I wanted to, and that it was up to me to choose what my life would become.

EXPLORING THE SPIRIT WORLD

Connecting to Spirit

I remember the first time I saw a spirit. It was completely unexpected, and I have to say it scared me so much I screamed the house down. I was about eighteen years old and still living with my parents. I recall seeing a rather large man standing at my bedroom door. I didn't have any contact with him other than seeing him. I jumped out of bed, turned on my light and he disappeared. Knowing what I know now, he was most likely still standing at my bedroom door, and I would have run right through him as I escaped. By the time I reached my parents' bedroom I was crying and my whole body was filled with fear. Thankfully my Mum calmed me down and told me that it was probably just a dream. Although that made me feel slightly better, because a part of me wanted to believe that ghosts weren't real, I knew the apparition I saw was not a dream.

Similarly, years later while on holiday with my then boyfriend, I saw a manifestation of a lady standing at the end of our bed. As in my previous encounter, I screamed and woke my boyfriend up. Although I explained to him what I had seen, I had no way to really understand what I was experiencing.

Over the years, I had many visits from spirits just like that first encounter. I gradually learned that there is nothing to fear about the spirit world. While we are physical beings, they are non-physical, which means we operate with a denser vibration or frequency.

I recall the first time I spoke to a spirit that I could see clairvoyantly (by using my extrasensory perception "ESP"). He was a teenager, who I knew very well, and who I'll identify as Ben. He had been a patient at Princess Margaret Children's Hospital, and the last time I saw him in the physical realm was while working at the SER.

It was the end of the day. I wandered down the tunnel painted in rainbow colours towards the elevator. As the doors were about to close, Ben put his hand out to stop the elevator door closing and got in with me. I remember thinking that this was strange because he wasn't allowed to leave the hospital; his second home was in ward 17 of the hospital, which was the ward for teenagers located right at the end of the rainbow tunnel on the same floor as the SER.

I asked him where he was going and he replied, "I'm just coming for the ride." Then he looked me in the eyes, gave me the biggest, warmest smile, and told me how much he liked hanging out and how he appreciated what we did in the Starlight room. I then got out of the elevator and he pressed the button to go back up to his ward. I felt it was an unusual, but heart-warming encounter. It was also the last time I saw Ben.

When I arrived at work the next day, there were teenagers crying. Ben had made his transition overnight. Although he had Cystic Fibrosis and was ill for a very long time, his passing was unexpected and came as a shock. It was surreal. But despite all the sadness on that day, I witnessed and experienced the presence of love all around me. I hugged more crying teenagers, parents and staff than I'd ever done before; it was a true expression of how much everyone loved and adored this young man.

The next morning, I booked a spiritual mentoring session with my Reiki Master, Jacqueline. I told her what had happened to Ben, and she asked me if I would like her to connect to the spirit world and to connect with Ben. Of course, I said, "yes" as I thought that she would be doing all the communicating between Ben and myself. However, that's not what happened.

Using spiritual mediumship, Jacqueline connected to the spirit world and started asking several questions with the intent of connecting to Ben. She called Ben through, and as soon as he came through, I could also see him clairvoyantly. He looked magnificent, exactly as he was in real life, but with absolute radiance. With a warm smile, he appeared calm and content. I told him how much he was adored by so many people, and that all his friends were devastated that he was no longer here with us in the physical world.

We spoke for about fifteen minutes. Although I can't recall what we talked about, communicating with Ben was pure evidence to me that his essence continued to exist, even though he was gone in physical form. Even if he had wanted to pass on messages to his loved ones, at the time I didn't have the confidence to relay them. I was still coming to terms with what I was personally experiencing. However, what I did gain was a deep knowing that the spirit of a soul continues after death. Ben's life force continued, but without the physical pain he had endured for most of his young life. He was free from such burdens. I didn't get a sense of any sadness or grief from him, but rather a feeling of absolute love and peace. All I can say is that seeing Ben and knowing that he was okay gave me the strength and compassion to support his friends over the weeks and months that followed. He was loved by many and will always hold a special place in my heart.

My interaction with Ben provided me with a sense of peace and made me realise I could move past my fear and communicate with the spirit world. My experience with Ben's spirit was a catalyst for my interest in studying mediumship for the next decade.

Meeting Anya and My Spirit Team

After my experience with Ben, I embarked on a four-year journey learning mediumship and spiritual development with Samantha. In our development circle, we were taught how to communicate with our spirit guides, guardians, and our deceased loved one's in our mind or out loud, as they are never far away. At the same time, we learned more about ourselves in the process.

When working with spirit, we always began the sessions by calling in the light and connecting with our guides. We referred to this as "sitting with our guide" - a very important exercise for anyone wanting to connect with spirit. While sitting in the power was about building up our energy and connecting with the spirit world, sitting with our guide was about establishing a deeper connection with our personal spirit guide. It was a process that involved quieting our minds and allowing space for our spiritual guides to come through with insights and wisdom. The messages we received needed to be delivered with love, kindness, and sincerity, and getting clear and accurate messages was our highest priority.

During our development circle, we also practiced sitting in the power, which involved building up our energy in our solar plexus and moving it up and out to connect with the spirit world. This exercise raised our vibration and allowed us to connect with spirit more easily.

It was important to make a distinction between sitting in the power and sitting with our guide. While they are both valuable exercises, they serve different purposes. It was also important that we could use meditation techniques to quiet our minds so we could be in a receptive state. Although I found these messages intriguing and often helpful, I couldn't shake the feeling that I was missing a crucial piece of information.

During one of our meditation sessions, I felt a sudden, strong presence in the room. It was as if someone was standing right next to me. When I opened my eyes, I saw nothing, but the feeling persisted. I closed my eyes again, and that's when I heard a voice in my mind. It was soft and gentle, yet firm and clear. The voice introduced itself as Anya, my spirit guide.

From that moment on, Anya became a regular presence in my meditations. She would often share messages of wisdom and guidance, and I always felt a sense of calm and reassurance in her presence. As I got to know her better, I learned that she was part of a team of spiritual beings who were here to support and guide me on my journey.

Through my connection with Anya, I learned more about myself and my spiritual path than I ever thought possible. She helped me to trust my intuition, to see the beauty and magic in the world around me, and to stay true to my authentic self. Our bond has only grown stronger over the years, and I know that I can always turn to her and her team for guidance and support.

As I developed over the years, my connection with Anya and my other Reiki healing guides provided me with the ability to channel high level guidance and spiritual wisdom and insights to my clients to help them find and create more joy in their lives. My initial workings with Anya would later turn into a love and passion for channelling her wisdom to others. However, at the same time, I brought through hundreds of passed loved ones to grieving clients, which gave both parties the opportunity to say what they needed or desired to say to each other. Such communications have provided solace and a sense of closure for those in grief.

During one of my classes, before doing a live demonstration of Intuitive Reiki, I asked the participants if anyone would like to be a volunteer to receive Reiki. A student,

Joanne, eagerly raised her hand as she wanted some guidance with respect to her spiritual journey as well as assistance in trusting her intuition. Before the demonstration began, I instructed the rest of the students to send love and Reiki to support the energy needed for the demonstration. I'm not usually aware of the direction a reading will take, however, in this instance, within a very short time, I could sense the presence of a male spirit. When I telepathically asked who he was, he identified himself as Joanne's father. I told Joanne that her father was present, and she immediately became overcome with emotion. He wanted her to know that he was very proud of the healing work she was undertaking and how grateful he was for her support as he made his transition. It was obvious that Joanne was still grieving the passing of her father, and hearing those messages helped her to process and release some of her grief. Joanne later mentioned to me that she had learned Reiki many years ago and that her decision to do so was so that she could use it to help her father feel more comfortable during his prolonged illness and eventual transition. She explained during the demonstration that she had experienced a huge shift in perspective; Joanne realised that learning Reiki this time around was about self-love and her spiritual journey. The connection with her father provided Joanne with huge comfort, knowing that he was still encouraging and supporting her to be her most joyful self, and to make the most of the opportunities presented to her.

Communicating with spirit does not always involve connecting to a human spirit but can transcend to connecting to the animal spirit world. I once worked with one of my Reiki students, Amanda, who told me that she was feeling extreme guilt over the tragic passing of her beloved horse. Amanda explained that she was extremely close to her horse and had personally cared for him for several years. After taking on additional commitments which resulted in her having less time with her animal friend, she eventually decided to move her horse to a new agistment centre to be cared by someone else. For several months, the new carer led Amanda to believe that her horse was getting the best care possible. However, she later discovered that her horse had been severely neglected, which led to his death. Since then, Amanda was filled with anger, guilt and resentment.

As Amanda explained her situation, I could feel the immense pain she was in, and I immediately wanted to help her to find peace and acceptance around how her horse had died. I began channelling Reiki, gently talking to Amanda to ensure she was feeling comfortable. I also asked her to state her intention to release the emotions she felt regarding the circumstances of her horse's death.

As I tuned into Amanda, her horse came through in spirit. I described what he looked like and tuned into his energy and the relationship Amanda had with him. Amanda immediately began to cry and validated that what I saw and felt was her horse. Her horse emanated such positive feelings and I could feel the immense love between them. The horse telepathically communicated the gratitude he had for Amanda, and he showed me visions of their life together and the love Amanda provided for him while in her care. No matter what transpired later in his life, he was aware of her love for him. Although the transition was difficult, Amanda's horse was no longer suffering once he had passed – a message Amanda needed to hear.

After the communication ended, Amanda felt a sense of relief and calm, knowing how her horse felt before and after he died. More importantly, she was able to forgive herself for the circumstances surrounding his death.

Know that when you say goodbye to those you love, although they are no longer physically with you, they can be with you the instant you call them into your awareness. We can all communicate with the spirit world with some training, but it is your intuition that is the key to unlocking the door to the spirit world; a key which every human is born with. If you choose to work on activating your intuition, you too can enjoy the benefits of both the physical and spiritual worlds. It can bring you a change of perspective, and create more love, light and joy in your life.

What is Channelling?

It's helpful to understand how channelling works and why you would want to consider learning how to channel. The term "channelling" is a general term that refers to communication with spirit. This means that there is a blending that takes place with the person channelling and the respective spirit. While studying mediumship, I was introduced to different methods of channelling, and I've provided a short description of a couple of the most popular methods below.

Conscious Channelling – This occurs when the person who is channelling spirit is aware of what transpires during the channelling session. During this type of channelling, a sense of depth and clarity is created which is beyond words to describe, as both the channel and spirit experience each of their respective worlds simultaneously. More significantly, the channel is able to experience two perspectives at the same time—their own as well as that of spirit.

Unconscious Channelling – This occurs when the person who is channelling steps entirely out of their waking consciousness when they channel. Some report that channelling is like falling asleep, such that when they return to their normal waking consciousness, they have no recollection of what was spoken through them.

When I was training as a psychic medium, I attended a week-long conference in Melbourne facilitated by two world renowned psychic mediums, Tony Stockwell and Lynn Probert. During the conference, Lynn explained that, in order to communicate with spirit, one must know the difference between working from the mind versus working from high level guidance. She explained that the mind or ego must take a back seat and that only through quietening the mind and "getting into the power," or raising one's vibration, can you then access the spiritual realm. To demonstrate the difference between the two, I will first describe a candle from my mind's perspective:

This candle that you can see has been used for generations to light a space. We can see that this candle is a soy candle. Did you know that soy candles burn clean energy and are much more pleasant and healthy for the environment? Lots of candles are also scented, which make them more enjoyable to work with when meditating and relaxing.

To demonstrate what it is like to communicate with spirit, I'll do the same now as I call in Anya:

Experience the stillness as you come back to the safety and the security of your own pure heart. A place of peace that can be experienced at any time with the simple intention to do so. This candle represents the one light, that when ignited, is filled with a passion for service, which can make such a difference in this world.

We are coming into a new time, and a new spiritual awakening has already taken place on this beautiful planet. The hearts and minds of the human beings that are inhabiting this earth have called for a resolution and the solution has arrived. It can be seen represented here so simply in the light that is gently pulsing from the candle. Through the light of this candle, one can instantly be reminded of humanity, love, kindness and compassion. One can recognise the positive qualities and true benefits of being here and now, while the planet is in this great wave of transformation. Be like this candle - move with ease and grace as you navigate your way through, knowing always that you are deeply loved and held in the arms of the beloved.

We hope you can feel the energy of love that we are transmitting and from the words you are now reading on this page, and may the love ripple out from here to there for all of time.

I channel consciously, and after my sessions with Marnie, life kept providing me further opportunity to fine tune my channelling ability. Although I loved channelling, I often compared myself to other world-class channels and felt inadequate; I was afraid of not bringing through clear and accurate messages. Suffice it to say, my confidence in channelling gradually grew through the practice of Reiki, offering channelled messages during both my Reiki sessions and classes. I eventually gained the confidence to teach others how to channel their own spirit guides, as well as to channel for public audiences.

Channelling Messages from Anya

I can recall my first experience channelling Anya as though it happened yesterday. During one of my Reiki classes. I was attuning a small group of students to the first level of Reiki. With each person I attuned, I could feel myself relaxing into a state of deep peace and joy. The more I focused on attuning each person, the more loved and expansive I felt, so much so that I had tears streaming down my face; it was a feeling of awe. Finally, as I was attuning the last person, I felt this wave of energy pass through my body, and the beat of my heart began to increase. The energy then intensified at the back of my neck, and the feeling was one of pure ecstasy. I knew it was Anya; it was as if she was standing next to me and talking to me telepathically. Her energy was also more intense than I had experienced before. I had been wanting to channel for a long time, and I felt that Anya had come through, because I was no longer afraid of my ability to channel and instead, had full trust in the process.

I heard Anya say to me very clearly that she had a message that she wanted to share directly with the group. I was given what I call a "download" of what she wanted to share. The download is difficult to explain, but it is akin to watching an inspiring and empowering movie. After the movie is over, I then have a vivid recollection of the movie/message to share with the group.

Anya wanted to talk to the class about the awakening they were going to experience through the Reiki energy. At first, I was hesitant to allow her to speak through me, but I knew in my heart that I had to surrender and take a leap of faith that what Anya would share would be far greater and meaningful than what I could have shared. So, I said "yes." Immediately, I felt a shift flow through my body, and being a conscious channel, I could feel her message. I felt a richness and an expanded state of consciousness where every word spoken held greater meaning. I was experiencing Anya's world and my own simultaneously, and it felt amazing.

This experience was the beginning of my channelling skills. I soon realised that aligning with and channelling this high frequency provides me access to infinite wisdom, which guides me and others at the same time. I also realised that learning and practising Reiki creates a wonderful foundation for channelling, as it establishes the perfect platform for me to clear my mind and get into a state of pure alignment with Source. It was a natural step for me to verbally express the pure loving energy that flows through me to inspire and assist my clients and students on their journey in a way that far surpasses what I can do through my own knowledge and experience. My desire to channel eventually led to working with healing guides and to inspirational speaking.

Developing Trust in Channelling

After my first experience channelling Anya, I continued to work with her. Although it took me some time to develop a deep trust with my guidance from Anya, after allowing her to come through during several of my classes, I became more confident. I eventually had a calling to offer live group channelling sessions to those who were interested in receiving messages from Anya. One group session in particular stands out in my mind.

I held the session in my healing centre one evening, and I was so nervous. Although it was one thing to channel Anya's messages while teaching, it was another thing to perform in front of a large, captive audience. I had done all the preparation and asked three of my trusted Reiki Masters, Fiona, Rachel and Venny, to support me at the event. The audience was due to arrive in a few hours, so beforehand, we walked to a local restaurant to have dinner. While we were waiting for our dinner to arrive, I started to explain to my Reiki Masters how anxious I was feeling, "What if I can't channel? I'm used to channelling with small groups while teaching Reiki. I'm afraid I won't be able to connect, and then I'll look like a weirdo."

When I had finished my rant about how afraid I was, my beautiful friend, Rachel, looked me in the eyes and said, "Lisa, the event is over now and it was a huge success. You were amazing – now eat your dinner." And just like that, my fear and anxiety dissipated. What followed was a lovely dinner before the time came to walk back to the centre to greet the audience as they started to arrive.

Before the event began, I meditated in my healing room with the door closed. I then called in Anya and asked her to channel a beautiful, empowering message for the group. When the event began, Venny introduced me and as I walked confidently to the front of the room, the first thing I noticed was a man sitting front and centre with his arms crossed, and not a hint of a smile on his face. My confidence immediately disappeared and fear struck. I started thinking, *He's been dragged to this event by his wife or partner and he really doesn't want to be here. But why would he be in the front and centre of this huge group? I bet he thinks I'm weird.*

Feeling myself beginning to spiral into a fit of anxiety, I begged Anya to help me. Immediately, I heard her calm, beautiful voice in my mind saying, "Don't judge this man based on how he is sitting. All who are here are open to your channelling. Focus on the others, if that makes it easier for you, Lisa. Focus on the people that you are here to help, rather than how you are being perceived by them." Wise words. So I shifted my chair so that I wasn't sitting directly in front of this man, and changed my focus.

The program began with Venny guiding the audience with a short meditation. During the meditation, everyone in the audience had closed their eyes, which gave me a sense of relief; for those few minutes, I wasn't the focus of their attention, which allowed me to ground myself and to get out of my head. My anxiety dissipated, and in a relaxed state, I called Anya through. Suddenly, I felt this powerful surge of energy move through my body, and I could see and hear more than I had ever done with clairvoyance or Reiki alone. It was as if all my senses had expanded a thousand times. A rush of energy flowed through my body, and I began to speak to the audience. I could hear my voice, however, it felt more fluid than normal. In addition, the choice of words and the way the words were put together were also different from my manner of speaking. I could hear every word Anya said, and as she spoke to the audience, I could see clairvoyantly, aspects of some of their respective lives. It was like watching a movie. As she focused on one person in the audience, the rest of the audience would fade out of focus. I would then receive and relay messages and images downloaded into my mind regarding the particular person in focus. Anya touched upon several people that evening, and provided messages to them, which hopefully served them well. In fact, many who attended said they felt that their questions were answered, even if they did not get a personal reading.

When the energy subsided and I came back into my own full and normal awareness, I felt like I had just been blessed. I felt uplifted and so amazing. The feedback I received was very positive, and I was proud of myself for stepping out of my comfort zone. The experience left me feeling both relieved and excited about the work Anya and I would do in the future.

After many years of channelling messages to my Reiki clients and during Intuitive Reiki live demonstrations, I have come to realise that Anya's messages not only resonate with a particular person, but the entire group in attendance. The guidance that comes through for one will usually benefit and bring insight and many "a-ha moments" to others. Many people have said that her messages are both inspiring and educational, and that they feel uplifted after the session. While honing my channelling skills, I have also found that if I connect with a person by putting my hand gently on their shoulder while I'm channelling, it occasionally creates a two-way link, which allows the person to sometimes feel and see through their mind's eye, the messages that Anya is communicating through me.

Over the years that Anya and I have been working together, I am proud to say that we have touched thousands of people's lives, through this incredible blending of the physical and non-physical realms.

CHANGING LIVES WITH INTUITIVE REIKI

I believe that learning and/or receiving Intuitive Reiki can completely change your life, or at the least, an aspect of your life. In my experience, I've seen how my clients and students view the world and how life events change through learning and/or receiving Intuitive Reiki. Many times, they move from a place of helplessness and despair to one of hope, love, and compassion.

I began this journey with a desire to learn and to have a greater understanding of what underpins the events and circumstances of our lives. What I discovered in the process was my calling and purpose in this lifetime – to empower and be of service to others so that they may live their most joyful and fulfilling life. Following are some experiences of my clients and students.

Kaitlyn

From Anger to Healing: Kaitlyn's Journey with Reiki.

I first met Kaitlyn as one of my Reiki 1 students. She was full of energy - a "straight shooter" with a wicked sense of humour. However, at the same time, she was filled with anger because she had been in a horrific car accident that had not only nearly ended her life, but had left her with a great deal of pain, and unable to work. She later confided in me that when she first signed up to learn Reiki, she was in despair and struggling to find reasons to keep on living. She had once been a very athletic woman and prided herself in her senior role working in the healthcare field, but in one moment, her life as she knew it was changed completely. As a result, she was broken in body, mind, and spirit.

Kaitlyn enrolled in my Intuitive Reiki course in hope that she would find some relief from her physical pain and emotional suffering, and find meaning in her life. Suffice it to say, she completed all levels of Reiki, including the masters' training, my channelling course and my private 1:1 spiritual mentoring program and learning. Kaitlyn developed her spiritual and intuitive ability, and was able to get accurate messages after completing my courses.

Over time, I noticed a huge shift take place within Kaitlyn. She came to accept, acknowledge, and release her anger. She healed on every level of her being and changed her perspective on life. She has since bought a new house and continues to enjoy practicing Reiki. In addition, she forged the most beautiful relationships with a small group of fellow Reiki students, who played a big part in her healing journey. Kaitlyn told me once that her Reiki friends were different to her other friends, she considered them her soul friends with whom she would love and stay connected for the rest of her life.

Candy

Candy released her fear and chose love and self-acceptance.

In 2015 I experienced two unexplained seizures that threw me into an absolute world of fear. I felt out of control in my own body. Not knowing what to do to prevent further seizures, I completely shut down and isolated myself from the world. As a consequence, I was no longer able to drive, swim, have a bath, drink alcohol, workout, overexert myself or go anywhere alone. For twelve months I put my life on hold and spiralled into depression and anxiety.

One morning while listening to a self-development podcast on my walk to the bus station, it became clear to me that there are two choices in life - love or fear. Living in fear of another seizure wasn't protecting me at all. In fact, it was keeping me from really living. I was simply existing. So, I started to commit to choose to love, and that is where I began connecting and exploring spirituality through learning Intuitive Reiki from Reiki 1, through to becoming an Intuitive Reiki Master.

Becoming attuned to Reiki set me on a new path and consequently, my life was forever changed. Dramatic shifts occurred within me. I began to unravel, release and heal from a twelve-year co-dependent relationship. Through this process I continued to paint, and I called upon a community of soul sisters to support me. After a lot of deep work on myself, later that year I entered into a new, healthy and loving relationship and went to India, taking five women with me and co-hosting a women's retreat - "Let go & Let India."

I felt the call to leave Australia in 2019 to return to my homeland, New Zealand, to let go of full-time work and to deeply commit to my purpose. Since then, I have been on one of the deepest journeys yet. Stepping into my soul work has been another evolution of self-mastery, awakening and opportunity for me to transcend the conditioned beliefs I hold about myself and to rise into being of greater service to my community.

I never found the cause of those seizures and to this day have not had any more. I consider those seizures to have been the impetus I needed to reconnect to myself and my hidden gifts, and to step into helping others.

Candy completed her Intuitive Reiki Master training in August 2016. She is an Intuitive Abstract Artist, Usui Reiki Master, writer, and all-round creative goddess. Her mission is to assist others to get out of co-dependency relationships, and to support them in finding their power, authentic selves, and purpose in life, love and sacred leadership.

Candyce Murrell

https://iamcandylove.com/candy-love

Linda

Linda found her voice and changed her life.

When I decided to embark on my healing journey, I was at the end of my tether. I had been in a difficult relationship for several years, one in which I never had a voice. I never told people how I felt or what I wanted. I never made choices for myself; instead, I succumbed to the needs of everyone around me, and pushed all my needs down into a bubble. I felt I wasn't deserving of happiness or good enough for anything. I was going through life with blinkers on, unable to see the world around me as a safe and happy place. As a consequence, I was on and off of anti-depressants for twenty-seven years.

I finally realised I couldn't keep going the way I was, and something had to change. So I began searching, but I wasn't sure what for. Then one day, while attending a book club meeting, a friend recommended that I try Reiki. I had never heard of Reiki before, so I did some research and found Lisa Brandis and Intuitive Reiki International.

I enrolled in the Intuitive Reiki workshops, which, initially, I found quite emotionally difficult; my head was so full of negative, self-sabotaging thoughts, keeping my mind open to other possibilities presented at the workshops was a challenge. However, as time went on, I gradually began to see who I was and how I wanted to be. In addition, I began having Reiki sessions with Reiki Master, Fay. I initially saw Fay weekly, but as time passed, I began to see you her less often - fortnightly, then every few weeks.

Having regular Reiki sessions with Fay was a huge help on a physical level, but especially on an emotional level. I had many transformational experiences during my sessions with

Fay. The sessions helped me to understand that I deserved to be happy and feel joy. Working with Fay gave me a sense of hope, and something to look forward to. She showed me that life didn't have to be this dark place and that it could be filled with light.

In addition, during this time in my life I went on a retreat to Bali. While in Bali, I had a fall and sustained a compressed fracture on my back. I was admitted to the hospital, and although I was in excruciating pain, I was given only Panadol, because I was allergic to other stronger pain relief medication. That's when I rang Fay and asked her to send me Reiki remotely. She sent me Reiki and I could feel the energy immediately, even though we were miles apart. After receiving Reiki, I was relatively pain free.

I learned Reiki in February 2018. Since then, my life has completely changed.

- *I am healthy, both mentally and physically, and have remained off of antidepressants for several years.*
- *I have a new job that I love and I work with people who I really enjoy working with.*
- *I am in a new relationship in which I can be myself.*
- *I have recovered fully from a fractured back and am pain free.*
- *And I'm excited to continue on my path of spiritual development knowing that there is always support in the beautiful Intuitive Reiki Community that I am a part of.*

Amber

After just one weekend – Amber walked away and her fibromyalgia symptoms all but miraculously disappeared.

When I was called to learn Intuitive Reiki, I had severe fibromyalgia symptoms. I was completely disconnected from my heart and I felt that life was a long, never-ending chore. I was very unhappy, and any moments of joy I did experience at that time were few and far between. I attended an Intuitive Reiki workshop with Lisa Brandis. I learned Reiki and my heart cracked wide open that weekend!

Before I took that class my entire world had imploded. After a series of events, I found myself a single mother to a one-year-old, had a hectic career and was dealing with complications that resulted in a near death experience. I had been battling for years just to survive and felt life was one long arduous chore. I had no joy and thoughts to end my life were constant for way too long. I tried everything to get help; traditional medications provided a band aid effect at times, but nothing was getting better.

I developed major fibromyalgia symptoms. Each week I got through my heavy workload by using pain killers, and getting chiropractic, physio, and acupuncture treatments. While all provided some short-term relief, the symptoms worsened and I had more painful days than pain free days. I remember calling my mum saying, "If I keep going like this, I'll be in a wheelchair in five years." I honestly felt like I was nearly disabled. It was scary, painful, hard, so hard, and so lonely.

I battled depression and anxiety and was in a lot of physical and emotional pain. I couldn't bear the thought of having to live like that for another fifty years. That's when I met Lisa at a course we were both attending. Lisa told me about her Reiki training and I decided to attend. I had no expectations and no real understanding of Reiki. I hadn't even had a session before. However, it just felt right, so I signed up for the course.

After attending the course over the weekend, my fibromyalgia symptoms all but miraculously disappeared! I couldn't have imagined that was even possible - and I didn't expect it. I quickly became a devoted student and continued to learn everything I could about Reiki. As a result of my journey with Reiki, I was able to love myself again. I stopped ignoring my needs and being a people pleaser. I stopped feeling so anxious and self-critical, and I was able to truly forgive those who had hurt me. I started to surround myself with people who were more balanced and connected to their soul's purpose. My world became lighter, brighter and I felt joy and hope again.

I've come a long way since my first Reiki workshop with Lisa. I am now a Reiki Master and teaching Reiki. I've now taught a range of people including nurses and a sceptical engineer, all of whom have had different, but amazing results. Reiki is a modality that I turn to in times of need for friends, family and myself. In my business, it is one of the primary tools I use for clients experiencing many different symptoms. I love being of service and to be back in alignment with my true authentic self, rather than stuck in the never-ending rat race and the comparison game.

Learning Reiki changed my life. Through Reiki and Lisa's guidance, I returned home to me, for which I am forever grateful.

Amber Harkins

Amber completed her Reiki Master training in 2016. She is an Empowerment Coach and Healer. Master in NLP, hypnotherapy, timeline healing, public speaker, DV and Suicide awareness advocate.

www.facebook.com/amberharkinslifecoach

Acknowledgments

Thanks to my business coach and friend, Marnie Lefevre, for making this book possible. Your belief in me and support helped me shine my light authentically.

To Eileen Cullen, my editor, thank you for guiding me through this process and ensuring my messages came across clearly. Your encouragement, direction and attention to detail helped me reach the finish line.

Athena Daniels, thank you for your support on my writing journey and for sharing your knowledge and wisdom.

Susanne Bellamy, my line editor, your expertise and patience made a huge difference as a first-time author. Thank you for your support and encouragement.

To my clients and students, I appreciate your trust and support on your journey of self-exploration. Special thanks to those who allowed me to share their story in this book.

Jacqueline Tuffnell, Tracy Willis, Rayeleen Gilbert, and Samantha Duly, my Reiki Masters and spiritual mentors, thank you for your guidance and love.

To my family, Gerald, Georgia & Hannah, Naomi and Andy Dawe, Reg and Stella Brandis, Craig, Leanne, and nephews Adam, Ryan, and Cody, thank you for your unconditional love and support.

Alicia Hagen, Fiona Greenlaw, Rachel Western, Robyn Martin, Burnella Rowecroft, Natalie Webb, Keryn Rose,

Michele Castle, Eleni Mitas, Kate De Jong, Sarah Doig, Ally Penfold, Amber Harkins, Candyce Murrell, Linda Stillitano, Wendy Holdaway, Lisa Webber, Julie Teshome, Jessika Zuks-Baker, and Venny Pages-Oliver, my Reiki colleagues and friends, thank you for your love and support over the years.

With heartfelt gratitude, I extend my thanks to you, the reader. Your decision to hold this book in your hands signifies a desire to grow and make a positive impact in the world. My greatest hope is that these pages empower you to trust your intuition, radiate love, light and compassion, and make the world a better place.

Resources

Social Links

https://www.facebook.com/intuitivereikiint/
https://www.instagram.com/intuitive_reiki_int
https://www.linkedin.com/in/lisabrandis/
https://www.youtube.com/c/LisaBrandis
https://intuitivereiki.com.au/

Events & Courses

Learn Intuitive Reiki:
https://intuitivereiki.com.au/learn-intuitive-reiki/

Learn To Channel:
https://intuitivereiki.com.au/channelling/

Upcoming Events:
https://intuitivereiki.com.au/events/

EXCLUSIVE BONUS MATERIAL

Looking for more inspiration and insight beyond the pages of this book? Sign up to my email list and receive a wealth of exclusive bonus material that didn't make it into the final edition.

Simply visit https://intuitivereiki.com.au/ and enter your details to gain instant access to a treasure trove of additional content. With regular updates and insights delivered directly to your inbox, you'll stay connected to the teachings and principles of Intuitive Reiki long after you've turned the final page.

Join me on this journey towards deeper understanding, greater intuition, and a more fulfilling life. Sign up today and start exploring the possibilities!

Index

1. Mysoor A. (2017 February 2). The Science Behind Intuition and How you can use it to get Ahead at Work. *Forbes Women.* https://www.forbes.com/sites/alexandramysoor/2017/02/02/the-science-behind-intuition-and-how-you-can-use-it-to-get-ahead-at-work/?sh=39b8877b239f

2. Petter, A, F. (2007). Understanding Byosen Scanning, Part II. *International Centre for Reiki Training.* https://www.reiki.org/articles/understanding-byosen-scanning-part-ii

3. HeartMath Institute. (2023), Expanding Our Capacity to Love. *Global Coherence Initiative.* https://www.heartmath.org/gci/

4. Sharkey L, Lamoreux K. (2021), What Does It Mean to Be Touch Starved? Healthline. https://www.healthline.com/health/touch-starved

5. Cleveland Clinic. (2020). Kangaroo Care. *Cleveland Clinic.* https://my.clevelandclinic.org/health/treatments/12578-kangaroo-care

6. Gur, T. (2023) Power vs. Fore: Summary Review & Takeaways. *Elevate society.* https://elevatesociety.com/takeaways-power-vs-force/

7. Davcevski, D. (2017). Here is What Each Finger on Your Hands Tells About Your Energy. Life coach code. https://www.lifecoachcode.com/2017/12/04/what-each-finger-on-your-hands-tells-about-your-energy/

About the Author

Lisa Brandis is an intuitive Reiki Master Channeller, author, and a leader in the field of personal transformation. She is the founder of Intuitive Reiki International. Over the past two decades Lisa has trained thousands of reiki and intuitive healers, inspiring them to trust their intuition and live empowered lives.

Australia's first Intuitive Reiki Master, and a Master of Masters, Lisa has spent the last two decades educating others how to make a difference in the world using the practice of Intuitive Reiki, a unique blend of Usui Reiki combined with an intuitive approach to healing and creating powerful change.

Lisa is a sought-after speaker for her unique approach to Reiki. Her dedication to mentoring and training practitioners worldwide has resulted in thousands of students creating thriving practices of their own.

Lisa lives in Perth, Western Australia with her husband, two kids, and two dogs, Rosie & Jesper. When she's not teaching or working in her private practice, she can be found camping with her family, reading a great book and travelling.

Head to https://intuitivereiki.com.au/ to learn more.

www.ingramcontent.com/pod-product-compliance
Lightning Source LLC
Chambersburg PA
CBHW050314010526
44107CB00055B/2240